Balancing the Rift: Re**CONNECT**ualizing the Pasenture

Balancing the Rift: Re**CONNECT**ualizing the Pasenture

IRUCKA AJANI EMBRY

Questioning the Universe Publishing (QUP)
Nashville, Tennessee, USA

"*peace. it does not mean to be in a place where there is no noise, trouble or hard work. it means to be in the midst of those things and still be calm in your heart.*"
–author unknown [quote found on a refrigerator magnet]

*Balancing the Rift: Re***CONNECT***ualizing the Pasenture,* First Edition
Irucka Ajani Embry

© Copyright 1993 – 2014 by Irucka Ajani Embry/the Questioner. Some rights reserved. This work is licensed under the Creative Commons Attribution-NoDerivatives 4.0 International License.

© Copyright 1993 – 1997 by the Questioner/Irucka Ajani Embry. Some rights reserved. Volume 1 was originally copyrighted as Creative Commons Attribution-NonCommercial-NoDerivs 3.0 Unported License (http://creativecommons.org/licenses/by-nd/3.0/) when it was published as an electronic book (e-book). The copyright has been updated for this work.

© Copyright 2012 – 2014 by Irucka Embry/Vibration Kunvorted. Some rights reserved. Excerpt of "Untitled" song off of the *What Do U Feel?* album by Vibration Kunvorted. This work is licensed under the Creative Commons Attribution-NoDerivatives 4.0 International License.

© Copyright 2011 – 2014 by Irucka Embry/Vibration Kunvorted. Some rights reserved. Excerpt of "Untitled: 20 bits" song off of the *What Do U Feel?* album by Vibration Kunvorted. This work is licensed under the Creative Commons Attribution-NoDerivatives 4.0 International License. To view a copy of this license, visit http://creativecommons.org/licenses/by-nd/4.0/.

Typeset in the following Free/Libre and Open Source Software (FLOSS) fonts: Lato, Alegreya Sans, Alegreya, Liberation Sans, Liberation Serif, FreeSerif, Charis SIL, Gentium Basic, and Gentium Book Basic

Printed in the United States of America

Published by Questioning the Universe Publishing (QUP), 2014
PO Box 68500
Nashville, TN 37206-8500
http://www.questionuniverse.com

ISBN-13: 978-0-9914994-0-3
ISBN-10: 0-9914994-0-9

Library of Congress Control Number: 2014901620

This book is dedicated to the Ancestors, to the Present, and to the Future which we are still sowing.

Table of Contents

Acknowledgments	viii
Dedication	xii
Preface	xiv
Volume 1: The Early Years (The Square Years): 1993 – 1997	1
A dedication to someone special (Original)	2
A dedication to someone special (Revised)	4
Love	6
Just For You	7
Phyllis Wheatley Peters	8
On Being Insane	9
Candy	10
A Ghetto Tale	11
A Walk Through the Forest	18
Un paseo a través el bosque	19
The Lover's Death	21
Volume 2: The Middle Years: 1998 – 2004	43
That Which is Within (Original)	44
Untitled: That Which is Within (Revised)	48
Untitled: Speakable contemplations about Detroit experiential	52
Untitled: Poesía en a different tunor	55
Untitled: Questioning the War Against the People of Iraq	60

Untitled: Inter- or In- dependence of People	62
Untitled: Peace and not the "War on Terrorism" after 11 September 2001	66
Familial Vibrations	68
Untitled: Questioning in tha Dream World	71
Nightmarish vision	93
A tour of the Empire	94
Warfare for the Future	101
Attack of the …	102
Dreamin' anew	106
Rumblings for the children	108
Fixability in a Brokable Fashionablement	110
Reflections on that which did not exist	111
Veritable emotional Quest	113
Sexual sensationality	114
Reflective Motherly vibrations	115
Magnificantlyness of Industrial Hemp	116
11 September: in Retrospection	118
Untitled: Us versus Them or People Screwing over Other People	119
Untitled: Did I say sexually frustrated?	124
Untitled: Alone and Angry?	128
Life in the Barrel	164
Untitled: Why I Chose Homeopathy	173
Untitled: 2004 Post Selection Thoughts	175
Untitled: Who am I?	178
Untitled: Religion ≠ Spirituality	189
Volume 3: The Great Years: 2005 – 2014	200
Untitled: Celebratory Uncles in tha mornin' dew of Life	201

Untitled: Climate Strange	206
Untitled: Prosaically delineating fortuitous gifts of virtue in a familial tonality	214
Rosacreatius	218
Untitled: Apologetically Urse	219
Momentous Musings in an Opinely Fabulent E-scale flatly G	223
Nucleated residues isotopically inundated in ounces of bullshit	225
Letting all the fucking juices hang out	227
Untitled: Controlled thoughts of random interactions aka What tha Fuck Was he Thinkin' Writing this Shit!	229
Untitled: The Sunset in Her Eyes	253
Myths in 2009 and Hopes for the Future	254
Say Goodbye to Poverty	260
Ending Food Deserts	262
Health for All of Us	263
Water for Life	264
Afterword	266
Appendix	272
Resourcical (R)Evolutionary Tacticals	273

Acknowledgments

Prayers and libations for the dearly departed.

How can I give thanks to all of the people that have made this book possible? I don't really know. I have thought long and hard for the past several months about how to make the perfect book. (For those that don't or didn't know, I'm a perfectionist when it comes to writing; however, I do take liberty with the grammatical chains from time to time). I wanted to put my best foot forward for this first book that I'm able to assemble.

I guess the only way to give proper thanks is just to say **THANK YOU** to everyone that has ever touched my Life, whether it was negative, positive, or a mixture of negativity and positivity. Without each of you this book would not have been possible.

Anyways, I would like to thank my lineage on both my father's and mother's side for giving me the heritage that has enabled me to speak up for what I believe is right and for passing along the gift of *true* education. I would like to thank the village that raised my siblings and me over the years. Thank you all soooooo much!!

I would like to thank all of my family, friends, associates, comrades, former (girl)friends, and other people (that I bestowed with other relationship labels) for being my guides along this journey that is Life. I would also like to thank all of the immaterial/spiritual guides that have provided me with my connections to the Past, Present, and Future (thus the conceptual framework of this work).

I would like to thank each of my teachers that I've had over the years for the encouragement, criticism, support, grammatical lessons, praise, and so on. In addition, I would like to thank those teachers that completed the initial editing for some of the pieces that you will be reading shortly.

And lastly I want to thank each and every one of you that will purchase this book, as well as any others that may read this book too.

This book is a step in the journey of my personal healing and transformation. I hope that this book provides both entertainment and useful information to you.

Thank you *all* again.

Over time I have re-realized that all Art can have many different interpretations for each person. I stumbled upon that lesson again during a class dialogue this past spring semester (2004) at the University of Tennessee, Knoxville (UT). I had enrolled in a graduate social work course, International Social Welfare and Sustainability, as I felt that that class would help me better understand Sustainability, which it did. Back to the aforementioned discussion.

In order to partially satisfy the course requirements on

Acknowledgments

the final project, I gave a brief lecture on the Web site [http://www.questionuniverse.com/oldway/crisis/crisis_home.html] that I had created. The subject of the Web site was the Crisis in Perception. [I credit Sharif Abdullah in *Creating a World That Works for All* and Fritjof Capra in *The Web of Life: A New Understanding of Living Systems* for fully discussing the Crisis in Perception and solutions to that overall problem. Thank you both and any others that have described this ultimate Crisis in their own ways.]

A few weeks before the presentation, I entered an exhibit in the Exhibition of Undergraduate Research and Creative Achievement Fair at UT. The exhibit consisted of a report, entitled "Sustainability: A Paradigm Shift in Engineering," and a poster depicting the old and the future paradigm of engineering design.

I used the aforementioned poster, created for the fair, as another teaching tool in my class presentation to illustrate how I defined Sustainability and the Crisis in Perception. I asked my classmates and the professor how they interpreted the poster, which depicted the Web of Life in stark contrast to the linear, mechanistic world that we have created. Each person gave their own idea of what they figured the poster represented. I, in turn, invalidated their responses that were different from my own vision of what I had created; however, since then, I came to re-realize that each interpretation of the poster was correct. There was no incorrect interpretation.

I now acknowledge that everyone will have a different interpretation of this book based on the time, space, place,

Acknowledgments

personal outlook, and so on of each "individual" person. As well, I recognize that I also have my own interpretations of why I wrote each piece and what they meant to me — when I conceived the idea and wrote the short story or poem & also now after years have gone by, in most cases. I bring this up, as I don't want you, the reader, to feel that your understanding of what I have written is somehow incorrect because it doesn't match any interpretations that I or others may have conceived. Each one of us must have our own view of the world.

Originally written in 2004 and slightly revised in 2014

Thank you to my family, immediate and extended, friends, acquaintances, and my good friend for your vocal and/or silent support.

Thank you especially to those individuals that have repeatedly asked when I was going to complete this book. Well, it's complete now.

January/February 2014

Dedication

This book is dedicated to

all Life in the Universes [Yes, that is right, I did mean to make the word "Universe" plural. There is more than one Universe. There are an unknown number of known and unknown Universes.}

Mother Earth/Father Sky.

to the worldwide Hip Hop Kulture.

all the poets, writers, sculptors, painters, musicians, singers, dancers, muralists, drawers/illustrators, dramatists/thespians /guerrilla theater artists, court jesters/fools, comedians, entertainers, activists, Lovers, Dreamers, Visionaries, Radical human beings, Revolutionaries, independently minded investigative journalists, metaphysicists, sacred geometrists, freedom/Truth Seekers, conscientious objectors to war /terrorism and other resisters to global domination/oppression, ecologists, healers of all forms, spiritual leaders and guides, organic and biodynamic farmers/gardeners, strugglers for freedom, and everyone else throughout the history of Time who have added their creative energy to the enhancement of Life for all of us on this one planet that we all share.

This book is also dedicated to the next SEVEN generations hoping that we will begin to heal and seek true Balance, Harmony, Inclusivity, and Peace with ourselves, with each other,

Dedication

with the Earth, our Mother & with the Sky, our Father.

Originally written in 2004 and slightly revised in 2014

Preface

Greetings and salutations! Welcome to *Balancing the Rift: ReCONNECTualizing the Pasenture*!

Where did the name come from? I conceived the name while thinking about the overlying theme of my Life: there is a rift within myself that I am working on balancing through the process of reconnecting my past, present, and future in the temporal continuum. There is also separation, within the world that we live in, that we must correct through reconnection, if we are to survive. Hence the name for this book. Re**CONNECT**ualizing was formed by replacing *concept* with *connect* in *conceptualizing*. Pasenture was formed by taking parts of **Pas**t, Pres**ent**, and F**ut**ure.

This is the first book written by Irucka Ajani Embry, though hopefully many more will follow.

\# Originally written in 2004 and slightly revised in 2014

Pasenture = Past + Present + Future = Now. Now is the only "time" that exists (although time is another one of those pesky illusions that we have been ill-conditioned to accept and believe). As you read this book, you will find thoughts on other illusions.

Preface

This book consists of 3 Volumes of chronologically arranged written expressions representing the following years: 1993 – 1997 (1), 1998 – 2004 (2), and 2005 – 2014 (3). This book consists of fiction and non-fiction pieces in the forms of poetry (rhyming and non-rhyming in narrative and free verse forms), short stories, and brief editorials (letters to the editor). It also contains 23 pages of useful book resources that will provide more insight into some of the ideas discussed throughout this work.

Most of the poems and short stories in this book veer away from the conventional modes of expression, so get prepared for the ride.

If you passed through the Table of Contents prior to arriving at this page, then I'm sure that you have noticed that I have used both the words: Fuck and Shit in some of the titles. Yes, I have used a variety of words in this work, including those that people may consider to be profane.

Vibration Kunvorted in his "Untitled: 20 bits" song, off of the *What Do U Feel?* album, offered these thoughts:

"2nd FUCK is obscenity / yet poverty / is acceptable / go 'head & eat these delectable / rhymes / in these misunderstood times."

Instead of ignoring the messenger because he or she uses words that society has deemed morally reprehensible, listen to the message of the messenger & question how any word can be considered to be immoral. David Icke, in the beginning of his

Preface

book, *Remember Who You Are*, offers a great discussion on this very topic.

    Enjoy your journey!

4 – 6, 12, and 15 February 2014

Volume 1: The Early Years (The Square Years):
1993–1997

A dedication to someone special (Original)

Baby, I want you
Right next to my heart
If I just can't, just can't have you,
Then I will totally fall apart.

When I see you everyday,
Honey I know you look fine
I really want to be with you
and hold you all the damn time.

I need you in my life
I just can't live without you
For all the things I do
I just wanna make love to you.
Maybe one day, I will make you my wife.

If I ask you for your love'n
and you tell me no
don't worry baby, I'll never let you go
I'll just keep a-buggin'

If I can't have you
I'll try, try, and try
and if you still don't want me
I just might cry.
By and by
I want you more, I love whatcha do.

A dedication to someone special (Original)

As I gaze into your eyes and peek at your gracious body,
I feel ashamed of myself so I run and hide.
I finally realized that I need you by my side,
But I look for you and you are gone.
I love your body
So that I wrote you this
Please don't dismiss
Me 'cause I can't take the pain of knowing how both of us feel on the inside
So baby, Will you be mine, 'cause that's how I feel on the inside.

A dedication to someone special (Revised)

Baby, I want you
Right next to my heart
If I just can't, just can't have you,
Then I will totally fall apart.

When I see you,
Honey I know you look fine
I really want to be with you
and hold you all the damn time
girl, you blow my mind.

I need you in my life
I just can't live without you
For all the things I do
I just wanna make love to you.
Maybe one day, I will make you my wife.

If I ask you for your love'n
and you tell me no
don't worry baby, I'll never let you go
I'll just keep a-buggin'

If I can't have you
I'll try, try, and try
and if you still don't want me
I just might cry.
By and by

A dedication to someone special (Revised)

I want you more, I love whatcha do.

As I gaze into your beautiful green eyes and peek at your gracious body,
I feel ashamed of myself and go run and hide.
I finally realized that I need you by my side,
But I look for you and you are gone.
I can't leave until I know that my feelings for you are known and done.
I love your body
So that I wrote you this
Please don't dismiss
Me 'cause I can't take the pain of knowing how both of us feel on the inside
So baby, Will you be mine, 'cause that's how I feel on the inside.

Love

What is love?
Is it something that you can
See, feel, or even taste?
What could love be, I ask myself?
Is it the way you feel about
Someone or something
Or is it something that you do
With other people on the weekends?
I believe love is the way
Your emotions are when
You are close to someone
That you care dearly about.

13 December 1993

Just For You

This poem is written just for you,
You ask who
Well, it happens to be you, my dear
[name deleted], you are special, one of a kind
so I had to snatch you up quickly and put you in my bind
I can't ever get you out of my mind
I fear
I may never see you again,
But where there is a will,
There is a way and our way has begun.
I do things just for you and for your love.
I would fly higher than a dove,
if I could just see you again and be with you for one day
And I don't even like heights or flying at all.
One day, we both will stand tall
Together and be happy once again.
Once again, this poem is just for you

Phyllis Wheatley Peters

Phyllis Wheatley Peters
A poet and an abolitionist
As a young child kidnapped from
Africa, her homeland,
Taken to Boston
Sold at a slave auction
wrote poetry at the age of 14
glad that she was brought to America
She was glad to be a Christian
Married John Peters
He was a grocer
They had 3 children
She was never really a healthy woman
She died on December 5
She died at an early age
She died when she was only
31 years old

10 May 1994

On Being Insane

On being insane
like a window pane
I was strapped in a strait-jacket
They had to beat me down wit a tennis racket
I had dreams of the world
burning in flames forever
I used to be sane
before I went
to a psychiatrist, I was bent
out of shape
I was a cannibal with no tape
to tape my mouth shut
with fear of rape, I tape
my mouth shut
You see my world is made up
of cuts
and I now have a fever
So shut-up
You sane

10 May 1994

Candy

Candy, it rhymes with dandy
So sweet in my
mouth by and by
I suck on it
to get all the flavas out of it
You can say
I have a sweet tooth, but I don't act that way
I love peppermints, candy bars,
and other kinds of candy
that I can eat
I love candy eats (beats)
Don't take my candy
It keeps me high
up in the air by my thighs
Candy

10 May 1994

A Ghetto Tale

Once upon a Time, in the city of Castrulonia, there lived some very, very, very poor people. {**The children were so poor that they had no clothes to wear, but their step-mothers were rich and had whatever they wanted.**} There were two couples that lived in the same apartment with their evil step-mothers. There lived Frothyist Waltkin and her husband Eyers Coloral and also Circuittous Composture and her husband Homolast Heteroflasken.

The step-mothers, Cinden Rellicen and Sping Whittlerst Trystnrey, made all four of them work **24-7 365**, thus they never had time to do anything fun. Their step-mothers ate up all of the food in their residence [*what little there was*] so that the husbands had to resort to shoplifting to get food to eat. If Eyers and Homolast ever got caught shoplifting, then their step-mothers would burn them alive and then bury them. So they knew that they had to be slick and live at the same time.

One day, a letter came from the Black House in Washington, D.C., it said that the step-mothers were invited to a ball. They were going to receive an award for being the evilest and meanest mothers in the whole universe. Of course, Cinden and Sping had to rub it in because they were invited to stay at the Black House for the rest of their lives. And their step-children would have to clean up their apartment and also the Black House everyday. It was their punishment for being born. If Eyers, Frothyist, Circuittous, and Homolast didn't do what they were told to do, then they would be turned to stone when they looked at the evil and ugly Spankiosk Mudadlrusa, dead in her eyes.

A Ghetto Tale

Cinden and Sping decided to leave for D.C. immediately after their step-children finished packing their bags, packing the car, making reservations at the Black House, and licking their feet too. The step-children had to lick their step-mother's feet everyday or that person would not be able to eat for three days. The children did as they were told, but then Cinden added a new chore for them to do.

She said, "I want all of you to wash my private parts with your tongues and then play with them."

Sping said, "I want you to do the same to me and lick my toes clean, because they haven't been washed **good** in over a year."

After the children did as they were told, they had to drive the step-mothers all the way to Washington, D.C., nonstop. The trip took them about three weeks.

Three weeks later...

The two families arrive at the Black House where they are greeted by the butler. His name is Bofritc and the bell boy's name is Bojjyic. Bojjyic offers to take the ladies' bags up to their room, but they refuse.

They say, "Our children can take our bags up to our rooms on the very top floor for us. It's only on the fiftieth floor, too bad there is no elevator for you **little peasants**."

Cinden and Sping go inside of the house and follow Bofritc

to the elevator.

      The two of them get on the elevator and head up to their floor. They get off the elevator and find the nearest room.

Sping says, "Boy am I tired from riding the elevator and watching them drive. I've done too much work today, already. I need to go up to my room and go back to sleep. Sleeping for about three weeks straight is not good enough."

Cinden says, "I agree with that, it's very true. WE beauties need our beauty rest." (THE IRONY IN THAT STATEMENT IS THAT BOTH OF THEM LOOK ALMOST AS BAD AS SPANKIOSK MUDADLRUSA. THEY THINK THAT THEY ARE THE MOST BEAUTIFUL THINGS IN THE UNIVERSE, BUT THEY ARE DEFINITELY WRONG.)

      Sping and Cinden break into the nearest room and they jump on the same bed at the same time. Sping lands on top of Cinden, but, luckily, neither one of them is hurt, if by some magic. Of course, that magic would have to be evil magic. Meanwhile, outside, Eyers, Frothyist, Homolast, and Circuittous, begin to carry the luggage up the fifty floors. Each of them take about ten bags and walk inside the crib.

They ask, "Where are the steps at?"

Bojjyic answers them, "Follow the black brick road and you will come to them."

A Ghetto Tale

Eyers says, "Follow me, I can take us there quickly, jump on my back when I turn into a magic carpet."

It took about thirty seconds for the transformation to occur and then all three of them jump on his back.

He flies straight to the steps and then he says, "Get off my back, we're at our destination."

All three of them jump off at the same time. Eyers, Frothyist, Circuittous, and Homolast walk up the stairs rather quickly, for the luggage is getting a little heavy for them. It took them about 6 hours to make it up to their step-mothers' room.

Cinden screams, "What took you **peasants** so long?!! You should have made it up here six hours ago!! What have you all been doing for all of this time?! You must be punished for doing what you all did! You must clean my arm pits and my feet, which haven't been cleaned in over two weeks! They smell like funky, raw sewage!"

Sping adds, "Yall know that you must use your tongues when you do it. You four need to clean me, too. After yall clean us, you can go park the car somewheres."

The children cleaned their step-mothers and then they took six hours to make it back down to the bottom floor.

Eyers said, "I will go outside and find a place to park our car, because it is late at night, right now. I don't want you three to be hurt or anything like that."

He walks to the door, opens it, and he looks outside. He is very astonished and surprised, somebody has taken every single piece of his car, even the out-of-state license plate. Eyers runs outside and tries to find a police officer. He finds none so he swears at *one-time* under his breath.

He says, "*One-time* is never around when you need them the most, but when you don't need them they're right there!!"

Instead of going up to tell his step-mother what has happened to his car, he decides to strangle himself to death. Frothyist, Circuittous, and Homolast hear him gagging and they run out to the street to see who it is dying. When Frothyist sees who it is, she falls down and then she faints. Circuittous picks up a piece of pipe and she beats the shit out of herself, Homolast does the same exact thing. A couple of minutes later, Frothyist awakens and she sees that her husband and that her two best friends have died. She begins to cry and then she thinks for a moment.

She says to herself, "I must kill my step-mother and Circuittous' step-mother, they deserve to die and not us."

Frothyist runs to the closest gun shop. She opens the door, walks in the store, and then she takes a Tech-9 that was on a rack. Frothyist runs out of the store as fast as she could. She runs to the Black House and she runs in through the front door.

She asks Bofritc, "Tell me where the fuckin' elevator is or I will blow off your freaking head!!"

Bofritc runs with Frothyist to the elevator.

Bofritc pushes the "up button" and it flashes. The elevator opens and then Bofritc and Frothyist rush onto the elevator. Frothyist pushes the button for the fiftieth floor. It takes about fifty seconds for the elevator to make it up there. Frothyist blows Bofritc's brains all over the elevator, because he was too slow. She runs towards her step-mother's room and then she halts for a moment. Frothyist must think of a plan to kill them, but how, they are too evil.

She continues to run to their room. She knocks down the door and then she starts pumping bullets into their sheets. Frothyist hears no words from the step-mothers, did she kill them once and for all or are they too powerful for her? Cinden lifts her head up from under the sheets. Her lips are soaking wet with saliva running down them and Frothyist knows exactly what she has been doing. Sping pulls the sheets off of them and Frothyist can see that both of them are butt-naked. Cinden's head was in Sping's deep and tantalizing, drenched pussy until she took it out.

Cinden and Sping kiss and then all Hell breaks loose. Everything in the universe disappears except for the two evil step-mothers and Frothyist.

Frothyist screams in anger and frustration, "Make my day, human rubbage, I'm gonna blow you two away!!! Yall goin' back to Hell, ya here!!"

Frothyist lifts her gun and points it at their eyes.

Sixteen million rounds of bullets later, we find Cinden and Sping in Hell and Frothyist is back in Castrulonia. After the two evil step-mothers were disposed of, Frothyist's fairy god-brotha and fairy god-sista came down to grant her one wish. She wished that her husband and her friends could be alive again and that she would wake up in her apartment. She is in her same apartment, but she has her husband back and her friends. When she killed the two evil, mean, and ugly things, almost everybody was born again. They live happily ever after or do they?

[Author's Note: I have made slight changes to the names of the characters and places since then. In addition, I've made some other slight grammatical changes. Even so I have tried to keep the original intent as much as possible through the revisions.]

This short story was written sometime between 1993 and 1995.

A Walk Through the Forest

One day, Hawantat and Ithical walk through the forest. They see a bunny on the forest floor. It is bloody and seems hurt.

She asks, "What can we do?"

I said, "We should take it with us."

I pick it up and we walk back to our house. I nurse the bunny back to health. We decide to let the rabbit rejoin its family in the forest. We cry at our departing with the rabbit. We are sad, we hope the rabbit makes it.

Time goes by... and we walk through the forest again. We see a rabbit that is limping. We think it is that one we saved. The rabbit hops toward us. I get down on my knees and it jumps into my arms. Hawantat follows and the rabbit jumps into her arms, too. We play with the rabbit. The rabbit hops the other way.

We follow the rabbit. It stops suddenly at a hole. It makes a noise and up comes another rabbit. We look down and see the bunnies. We are so happy.

THE END

Un paseo a través el bosque
Spanish translation of *A Walk Through the Forest*

Un día, Hawantat e Ithical dan un paseo a través el bosque. Ellos ven un conejillo que está sangrando y parece estar herido.

Ella le pregunta, <<¿Qué podemos hacer?>>

Yo le dije, <<Podemos tomar el conejo.>>

Yo lo cojo de arriba y nosotros lo llevamos a nuestra casa. Lo alimentamos al conejillo para que se mejore. Después lo traeremos para que se reúna con su familia en el bosque. Lloramos mucho cuando el conejo se marchó. Estamos tristes, esperamos verlo alqun día.

El tiempo paso... y paseamos a través del bosque otra vez. Vemos un conejo está cojeando. Pensamos que es el conejo que salvamos. El conejo brinca hacia nosotros. Yo me agacho y el salta dentro de mis brazos. Hawantat sigue y el conejo brinca a sus brazos también. Nosotros jugamos con el conejo. El conejo brinca hacia un hoyo.

Lo seguimos cuando llega al hoyo. Un ruido nos asunta del hoyo sale otro conejo. Miramos hacia abajo dos lindos conejitos nos miran. Estamos muy felices.

EL FIN

Un paseo a través el bosque

[Author's Note: A former college professor greatly assisted in the proper translation of this short narrative. Thank you very much. Muchas gracias.]

The Lover's Death

One that loved not wisely, but too well.

    This melancholy day passed by slowly and all that could be seen through the windows was a complete and utter darkness. A dark gray hue that had never before been seen by human eyes abruptly appeared out of nowhere. Outside, through the windows, nothing could be seen due to the dense gray substantiality surrounding the town. On this particular day, there wasn't a happy smile on anyone's face, and some feared that this was the end of the world already.

    Some people just didn't care what it was; they just went on with their tiresome lives as if everything was cool. However, there were a couple of folks that didn't know what was going on in the community at all and really didn't care, either. They just wanted to be left alone and sleep in the whole day. And on top of all that there was a thunderstorm on the way to this small town in the middle of nowhere. This sudden overwhelming darkness and storm front surprised even the most astute of those peculiar people, for today was to be a pretty day and there were to be no clouds on the horizon, only the sun shining brightly in the vast blue sky. But, it was nothing like that on this day. No one left their house and all of the businesses were closed on this day. Something very irregular had happened the night before; an odd, loud sound had been heard earlier that day. Some people in the municipality thought it was a sonic boom as there was railroad work being done not too far from there. However, I don't think they were prepared for what would happen to them, do you?

The Lover's Death

    Anyways, back to the city. This condemned community, for some bizarre reason, has more acreage of land allotted for cemeteries than they have acreage of total land in the rest of the city combined. The town (I think that it's too little to be called a city) has about 5 different families that originated in the minute municipality that came before it. The rest of the population came after the gold rush some time ago.

    What I still don't understand is why the domain of the cemetery plots are still registered under the name of a man who has been dead for a long time, well about 10 years or so. (That's more than long enough too done gotten a new owner by now.) Anyways, his name was Rufus Jaclyn Worshington. That name was given to him by the town council after he did some heroic deeds back in the day. Some say that he deserves the appellation, Sir or Lord; while many others think he deserves no respect whatsoever. Some members of the commonalty truly believe that he is the root cause of the gloomy day that exists today in Deathville. An appropriate name, don't ya think? I'll get back to why this day was so extraordinary.

    Of course, the people in Deathville had a good reason not to step outside on this dark and dreary day, for they only had electricity in their houses and had no kind of outside lighting. This community was slowly developing and day by day this place was also becoming more gruesome and deathly. To this very day there have been 25 unexplained, anomalous deaths and there have been many a missing people since that man, Rufus, died. Nobody knew much about Rufus, except that he was a nice and caring man so the ones that ever met him felt. That's all that he let people know about him; he seemed to be fairly introverted about his own life. But other than that, he wasn't shy or anything. Just plain enigmatic, yes indeed, he had eccentric habits and everything. He kept to himself totally when it was about his personal life and problems. Rufus developed an outer shell around himself. Not many people were brave enough to find out more about that old fool, cause ya see, he was strange; so odd that we were all scared of him, but that didn't stop us from wanting to know more about him though.

      Another thing that I can say about Rufus was that he was very munificent. Every penny that he got, he donated it to Deathville. And in his will he bequeathed all of his property to the municipality. He was always trying to help someone with their problems.

      One noteworthy night, I remember that I was over his house and we were discussing how to improve this place.

The conversation went like this:

"So, what do you think we should do about all of the land we have allotted for cemeteries?"

"Well, I don't know."

"Why did you pick this location to settle this community? Isn't it peculiar that this commonalty is surrounded by forests that no one is brave enough to enter and we have a huge graveyard, yet an extremely small population?"

I finished my sentence, and I looked around. I couldn't see Rufus. Where could he be? I know that I was just talking to him. He was just right there no more than 30 seconds ago. What did I say to make him want to leave? What did I do? Where could he have gone so quickly and quietly? I know that I could have heard him, if he was walking on the floor. These wooden planks have been here since the house was built and they look more rotten and deteriorated as the weeks go by, just like Rufus. They get weaker as time goes by too.

So I got up and went looking for him throughout the house. First, I checked his bedroom, however he wasn't in there. All that I saw in that room was a note on the floor. When I first arrived at his house he showed me his bedroom and there was a bed, a mirror, and a closet in there. Now, there's nothing in there except a note. Something very atypical is going on around here. Whereas I heard some abnormal noises outside, the sojourn at Rufus' house didn't last long at all. I had to leave the place as my sanity was no longer safe there. (I was supposed to stay there overnight or as long as I wanted to with him, however that was no longer a thought in my mind.)

I went back to my own house. I walked up the steps and the front door opened halfway on its own. No one was in the house when I left and no one seemed to be in there when I returned.

"Hello, is anyone there? Who are you? What do you want? I won't hurt you."

There was no answer, just the creaking of the wooden floor in the backroom. I cautiously and carefully pushed the already opened door the rest of the way, while simultaneously looking all around the house as I walked on in. As the creaking of the floor got louder and seemed to get closer to me, I felt a cold chill come over my body. A clatter that sort of sounded like the rattling of some rusty chains in the night mixed with a raspy, low pitched voice.

"Who goes there? What do you want?"

Once again, there was no reply. I could also hear the thunder outside. Oh what great luck, a thunderstorm is coming and I'm already scared. But I don't know. When I become afraid I seem to hear and see things that aren't really there. The adrenaline in my body started to increase substantially and go through its cycle. As that happened my body began perspiring buckets of water, literally. My whole body seemed to be drenched in sweat. I didn't know what to do or what to think or anything. I just had to know what it was that was frightening me so terribly.

Instantaneously, a foggy, cloud-like thick mist appeared out of nowhere throughout the house. The door closed suddenly behind me by itself and the deadbolt locked. I turned around quickly only to see a closed door. All that I could see was the door; nothing else could be seen by my eyes. All of the lights went out suddenly as if someone or something cut the electrical wiring.

The creaking that was getting louder stopped abruptly

and I heard an eerie, hysterical, strange laugh.

"HA!! HA!! HA!! UH! OOH!! HA!!"

    I was scared and didn't know what to do. I had only heard that laugh once before and it was when I was in the company of Rufus. It was his laugh. However, I knew it couldn't have been Rufus as all of the windows and doors were locked when I left out earlier to visit him. And there was no other way into my house, well, except for the cellar tunnel that I had built underneath the house. That tunnel commences at the cemetery and ends under my house. Don't ask why I did that, I just had to.

    I gingerly walked towards the laughing sound that I heard, casually walking, keeping my cool, trying not to make any noise at all. Actually, I tried to walk as quiet as a mouse, if I could, but sometimes it's hard to do so with your adrenaline rushing and your heart beating hastily. I finally got to the spot where I heard the laughing and I slowly stepped up one step. I fell.

    At that moment, I knew that I was not in the midst of humans, but in the presence of supernatural beings. The trepidation that followed my fall caused me to cry, for I dreaded that my own death was near and it made my fear increase. I became more alarmed and apprehensive of what was around me and in my house. I couldn't catch my breath. I tried to breathe, but nothing happened. It felt like my chest was caving in from the inside out, bit by bit. I felt chest pains, and my heart started beating faster and faster. Until.

Out of the blue, a piercing-taloned hand reached up from under one of the boards of the floor. The claws ripped through my clothes and bore into my skin. I couldn't believe it. I felt no pain. It was like I was completely numb. And there didn't seem to be any blood flowing from my open wound. The other hand started edging its way up through the plank that was directly under my posterior. I heard the deafening, uncanny scratching of the long claws on the wooden floor (like someone scraping a chalk board with their sharp fingernails). As the intonation got louder and louder, my heart started to beat faster and then skip beats in a synchronizing fashion. I couldn't move, I was horrified out of my mind, and I just wanted to die an easy death. I didn't want to go out like this.

"Stop it, whatever you are! Leave me alone!! I haven't done anything wrong!! I can't go yet! I don't wanna go!! Oh, God, please hear my cries!! Why have you sent him after me? I changed! I really changed this time! I've been good! I haven't done anything wrong! You promised me God! Why did you have to betray me?!"

Still, the second taloned hand pushed away the plank from underneath my back. I could feel the draft that was coming from the cellar tunnel. I could tell that this claw was sharper and that it could actually hurt me or even tear my frame to pieces. I smelled the blood that was on the second set of talons. I could smell it distinctly. I knew that it was not human blood, but it was blood nonetheless. I just couldn't remember what kind of blood it was, though, at that time. I could tell that the claws didn't belong to a paw or anything with hair on it, or else I would have smelled it. As my heart started beating more rapidly, my senses became more acute than they had ever been in my entire life. I started sweating profusely and the crying started and then I just couldn't say a word. I could open my mouth, but no matter how hard I tried, I just couldn't talk. I was really stunned.

I felt one of the claws beginning to dig a large hole in my posterior. The talon tore the skin off of my back. I mean all of it, not just some of it. Then, the 2nd claw started to rip the second layer of skin (dermis layer) from my back. Once this second hand touched my back, my body succumbed to its ultimate control and force.

My bones seemed to be vaporized and my vital organs exited my torso, all of them except for my heart. It was all that was left that was essential to my body. I couldn't stop it, it just happened. I had no power of my own to try to stop it or slow it down. Finally, the talon commenced tearing at what was left on my back. The claw stopped rending the small pieces of my clothes and putting them into different sections. Both of the hands started shining, and one of the claws reached up through my backside and reached for my heart. It moved out of the way of the talon; however the claw eviscerated a large hole on the other side of my body. Then, the other claw dug an even larger hole in a side of my body and started to work its gradual way to my heart.

The two claws reached for the heart at the same time. The two talons grasped it and squeezed it till it was so emaciated that you could use what was formerly my heart as thread. All that I could hear was the steady slurping of blood. Yes, the blood that was previously circulating around my body.

"Give me more blood!!"

"No, why don't you just stop it!! What has possessed you to be such an evil demon?"

    It didn't respond. It stuck a talon into the back of my head and started twisting it and twisting it. I was in some serious pain and didn't really know what to do. When you are in that much pain, you can't feel it at all, because your body is numbing itself. Preparing for the relentless decay when death comes knocking on the door.

    I could feel their red claws crushing my heart and ripping my whole body asunder from the inside out. I couldn't stop them, yet I didn't care that they were doing it. I don't know. The lurid description of my first death caused me to go into my other character and forget all that happened after my eyes closed. The description that was in my mind was so vivid and real that my brain couldn't take any more and relinquished my body to whatever it was that was attacking me.

    My eyes closed little by little and I was no longer there anymore. I awoke the next morning on a comfortable, king-size bed. And I didn't remember anything else from the night before. I woke up in a different body and in a different juncture of time, space, and place. This was a body that I knew nothing about as it was not mine.

The Lover's Death

"God, what has happened to my body? What happened? This is not my voice. I sound like a baby. What happened to my voice?"

Well, *this* body was stronger than the previous body that I had so I was satisfied about that part, at least. I pulled the black cover and the black sheets off of this body. I rolled over progressively to the edge of the bed, and I fell off. I hit the concrete floor, yet I felt no pain. I didn't feel anything. I got up and walked around. I had never seen *this* place before. Where in the world could I be? In my search for the bathroom, if there was one, I scrutinized what else was in this place. I didn't leave a single nook or cranny unseen or untouched.

I looked up at the ceiling for a quick second, and I stumbled over some large, glistening object on the floor. I lifted my head up and looked down towards my feet. I had on high-heeled shoes and my once hairy legs were now cleanly shaved. What happened? Whose body do I have?

Under my legs was a sizable looking glass. The mirror was spotless, without scratches on it, even though I just stepped on it. I determined that it was a magical looking glass and decided to pick it up off the floor. I grabbed one end of it with one hand and the other hand I placed under the other end. The mirror was raised off the floor in one instant. I looked into it, but I didn't see the body that I saw with my own eyes. I saw something evil. It was not even my reflection. When I moved this body the reflection stayed still and when I stayed still the reflection made its own motions. I looked at the countenance in the looking glass and I stepped back about 3 feet. I only saw that half-smile, half-frown, wry before on one person and that was Rufus. Only he could make that expression with his face. Only he could do it, he told us that himself. It was not that the expression scared me or anything like that, but I just hadn't seen it in so long that I had to check it out to see for myself if it was true or not.

    I felt a trepidancy overcome my body as the reflection in the mirror stared into my eyes and I stared back into its eyes and once again, a cold chill went through me. I saw its life through its eyes. Everything that I saw through it had happened to me. Was it my mind just playing tricks on me again? The reflection in the mirror opened its mouth like it hadn't been opened in years, or possibly even in centuries. The lips spread apart slowly and no noise came from the reflection. It tried again and again, until finally on the 100th time, I heard a loud shriek emanating from the reflection in the looking glass. I could finally hear its voice. It told me that everything that had happened to my other body happened to it too, and that I was in a time portal through the afterlife. I was neither dead nor alive; I was somewhere in-between all of that.

    As it continued to speak to me, a luminousness of crimson red appeared in its eyes. The red started to glow like some demon was engulfing his body, however there were no sounds from the mirror, except his continued chattering. Its eyes went from a regular tint to the brightness of the sun. It was all just too outlandish and different for me. It was so bright that it nearly blinded me. As it continued to talk, it became brighter and brighter, until its whole body was swallowed up in a fiery red flame of light. It was not fire or anything like that, but it was a ball of fiery light. As it continued to speak, its words became jumbled and it was like it was starting to speak in a different language

The Lover's Death

with different dialects and accents for each word it used. Was I still dreaming or what?

The exorcism that was happening to the reflection was so prodigious that I was lifted off of my feet and I was floating in midair without any known cause. It was like something or someone lifted me from the ground and into the air, except it was nothing like that at all. It told me in its last decipherable sentence that I would feel an anxiety since I was being transported back to the present-time. Also, I would have to view my death again. I began to feel tremulous as my body abruptly went cold and all motion stopped. It was like I was in a coma, but I wasn't. I just couldn't feel any other way except that way. My body began to shiver and that was the only motion that was allowed as my old body was being transformed to suit the new conditions and the new day. What it said to me became so much of a proxility that I became so bored with it that I fell asleep. And I didn't wake up even as his frigid, pale hands touched me on my forehead.

I awoke on the day that was described at the beginning of my narrative of my life in Deathville. To everyone else in the locale I have been there as myself in my own body and participated in the history that I, myself, missed. I felt that I had missed everything. I found out about all that had occurred while the other half was gone when both halves of my body transformed one into another. I put my thoughts together while I was still asleep in the present-time in Deathville.

I opened my eyes and looked at myself, I had the body that I had before all of this stuff happened and I could see that my body had been totally stitched back together and that the stitches were close to being gone for good. I believe that it's been many years since Rufus' death and since the attack. I looked around at all of my surroundings and I was back in the little brown, hardwood shack that I call my home. Instantly, there was a loud knock at the door.

It sounded like the person was beating urgently on the door, so I hurried myself up and went to see who it was. (I still haven't figured out that there is a total darkness encompassing the vicinity and that no one will leave their house today. I am getting a visit from something that is unheard of.) The door is opened gradually. As that happens the hinges of the door come a-loose and it makes a sharp, squeaky noise. I ask who it is at the door as the door is pushed wide open with force and quickness. I am now staring into the eyes of a ghastly looking phantom. The phantasm walks through my body and all I feel is just the draft coming from the open door. (I still haven't figured out about the darkness that has covered Deathville.) The door closed on its own. As I didn't do it I decided I would ask the phantom if it closed the door.

"Phantasm, did you close this door?"

"No, I didn't close that door; it must have been something else. Don't worry; you're safe as long as I'm around here."

"Well move closer over here and metamorphorsize yourself into something that I can see, alright!!"

"I guess that I could do that for you. I must complete my mission anyway. I will be your doctor for today."

As those final words were said by the phantom, a small explosion was heard within the house and a bright crimson red light appeared right in front of me. The phantasm was transposing itself into a human form and the small explosion was the way that it had to become human. [Please note that the words: he, him, it, the doctor, the good doctor, the great doctor, phantasm, and phantom all refer to the same entity throughout the rest of this narrative, unless otherwise used for Rufus.]

The doctor informed me that it was going to check me over to see if the stitches could finally be taken out, for they had been in my body for over 10 years. I was glad that I was being caught up on a lot of things about my body and stuff. I conversed with the doctor about how an odd, supernatural being tried to annihilate me by trying to squeeze my body from the inside out and crush my heart. Luckily, my heart is so icy and empty that they really had no effect on me, except some deep gashes and other bodily damage. Besides that, I felt great and still do. At least I think that I do. Too bad they weren't planning on me being more of a power than they or anyone or anything ever expected or could have. I really blew their minds and my own.

The good doctor let me know that after all of the stitches were taken out that I would be in a catatonic state until further notice and that it would only be a slight malady for my body. However, I should be alright, just very weak. I would be alright after I got used to not being able to move or anything like that. I would just be helpless like a newborn baby.

Another thing about good ol' Rufus was that he was a fervid person even though he rarely showed any facial expressions. He never showed a negative disposition to anyone, even if they had made him upset in some way or something like that. On the other hand, his smile was cunning and deceiving. He was always happy and loved to live, even though his face never showed how he really felt inside. He was always giving up his time freely to help out other people if they had problems or if the municipality itself had any problems. Rufus' abhorrence to the mention of religion or God is probably the reason why I was the only friend that he had and though he did a lot to help out this town he was still an outcast, an outsider.

Whenever the word religion was mentioned around him he would break out in a sweat and he would seriously commence perspiring crimson red drops of blood. His body would spew blood because of a word that was said. I said that he was unusual.

I asked the doctor not to sedate me before he got out his medical equipment and supplies, for my instincts told me not to trust it. The doctor ignored my wish and put me to sleep anyway. It stuck a large, silver needle into my leg and then pushed down on the bottom of the syringe forcing the freezing liquid into my legs faster than a speeding bullet. The liquid immediately began to put the bottom half of my body to sleep. After 5 minutes, the doctor stuck another needle into my arm next to a set of stitches. I opened my mouth and started screaming and cursing.

The doctor responded: "I thought I put you to sleep for good. I used more than the maximum dosage of this medication. What's the matter with you? Is your body so anomalous that its immune systems will withstand a dosage high enough to put a super strong, supernatural man to sleep for good? Why can't you be like other humans and be weak like them? You are not a normal human any more. Look at these stitches!! They're popping out on their own!!"

Just as he was saying that, about a thousand stitches began popping out of my epidermis and flying all over the place. Most of them ended up going through the good doctor's body and into the back wall of my bedroom.

It reported that when my legs regained feeling that they would not last much longer, maybe just a few minutes longer. Since most of the dosage was placed in my legs, they will become extremely weak and vulnerable to any diseases or practically anything. So my legs would become transient in a short time before the rest of my body passes away into dust and goes back to Nature. He told me that I could get some new legs if I went to the cemetery and took them from any person that I wanted to. I consented. I let him know that I would do that at night. He informed me that as my legs deteriorated that gangrene would form around the upper parts of my legs and my feet. However, as an alleviation for any pain that could occur, he would give me an even more powerful drug to get rid of my problems. I agreed with what he said. The doctor gave me the drug immediately.

I could feel the effects of the drug and the pain simultaneously and the two combined synergistically caused me much discomfort. I started screaming again and I even started crying, but the pain wouldn't stop. It just became more and more excruciating until finally both of my legs just pulled themselves away from the rest of my body and went out through the wall. I just couldn't believe it; they went right through the wall. The wall didn't break or anything like that though. It was like the wall was transparent and my legs were ghosts or something of that sort.

The great doctor commented: "Son, the phenomenon that has just occurred is inexplicable because there is no earthly reason why your legs left your body in that way. You're still human so that can't possibly happen, or can it? I really don't know what to say about what we just saw. Just ignore it and hopefully no one else saw it or would say anything about it. Just keep it between us son."

    During the rest of the day I continued to talk to the good doctor. I still didn't notice the outside. At midnight that night, I got out of the bed and thanked the doctor. I walked over about three or four steps from my bed. I knelt down on my hands and the nubs that were left. I lifted up enough planks of wood so that my body could get through. I fell down the rest of the way through the hole. It seemed to be a longer fall than it ever had been before. It was totally pitch dark in that cellar tunnel; it had never been that dark before. I didn't pay much attention to it though. Finally, I hit the bottom of the tunnel. I got up on my hands and started crawling towards the entrance. I just felt my way through the cellar tunnel because it was too dark to see anything. And it was oddly quiet in that tunnel that day; usually all I hear is noise in that tunnel, but I guess today was a different day.

The Lover's Death

I didn't pay much attention to that either. I kept on crawling until I reached a dead end. I knew that my body was covered with dirt and mud, but I couldn't really do anything about it. So I just carried on. I just started digging upwards because I couldn't go through the concrete dead end. I felt around the cellar tunnel to see what everything was and to see if anything was falling on me or anything like that.

I threw the extra dirt behind me. The mound of dirt that slowly formed underneath me helped propel me to the ground surface. Eventually the last handful of dirt is thrown under me and I am in the middle of the cemetery. I look right in front of me. I see the good doctor that was helping me. He is going back into his grave. I crawl over to his epitaph to see what was written. I read it; it was the epitaph that was written for the father that I never knew. How could it be though? This doctor is not my father. So why is he in my father's coffin? I must talk to him to see why.

The doctor came back up through the ground and started talking to me in a distinct dialect that I was able to understand. The doctor informed me that it was my father and that it died before I was even born. But I couldn't believe it.

"Why... why... why did you leave us? Didn't you love me enough to stay around for me?"

It replied, "Rufus... Rufus, that demon, killed me! I don't know what it did to me, but it wanted to get rid of you too. But I sent for you and helped you avoid your death then, however now you're on your own. Rufus will be back tonight with the rest of the demons to collect your body (corporeal body, mind, and soul). It would be easier if you just succumb to their powers. Look at your epitaph! Today is the day that you die! There is nothing you can do about it. Bye son! Today is the day that our love is joined and the day that death takes away our love for each other too. I didn't love you enough to tell you before. I knew that you wouldn't come here if you knew everything. Now you do! Go on son!"

That man was so importunate in the way that he declared that he was my father and that my life was in danger that I actually started to believe him. Silly me. I just turned and started to walk away. The thunder started up again, it got louder as each second went by. There was also lightning in the distance.

"Son, you must believe me! You will be the last one! It is our fate; it was set for the whole clan when I was born. You can't deny the 'Grim Reaper' his souls! You know that! Don't you son?! You can't escape the madness that I've caused you to live in! It's not my fault. I had to do it, son! He was gonna hurt you!"

"Who... who wanted to do all of this to me? Who was it?! Why don't you tell me who it was?!"

I heard no answer, so I just assumed that he was gone, forever. And it was the end of my own life as I knew it.

The next thing you know, everything is totally dark and nothing can be seen. I heard a high-pitched voice and then a low-

The Lover's Death

pitched voice and then back again for a minute or two. Soon it became discernible enough that I recognized it as Rufus' voice. It seemed like he was attempting to throw his voice around the empty cemetery to make me feel that I was surrounded. This time I held my ground and I wasn't even panicky at all. That was until hands came up from below the ground and started grabbing at me.

"What do you want with me?! I haven't done anything wrong! I thought we were friends!"

"Well, you were wrong and you need to learn how to pick better friends!"

He started that hideous laugh again; it was that hideous laugh that petrified me so horrendously before and it was starting up again. My heart started pounding and sweat came down like a torrential rainstorm off of my body.

The hands began tearing my body asunder limb from limb from the nubs of my legs up to my head. Then came the demon vultures. They started pecking away at my separated torso. All that remained when the hands stopped ripping me apart and the vultures stopped pecking insidiously at me was my carcass, but that wasn't good enough. Next came Rufus, he came up to me and kicked me dead in my ribs. I was now fleshless and I was closer to dying than I had ever been before. My ribs broke apart and flew far away from each other.

Rufus called on the hound dogs to take all of my bones

away. They did. A whirlpool instantly appeared in the middle of the cemetery, gathered up my other remains, and carried them away. The whirlpool came up from the doctor's grave. It sent me a message, loud and clear, yet it was too late. (It appears that one of Rufus' dogs died during this time period, although it is not exactly clear how this happened.)

Rufus, a known alto, began singing a song. It was a dirge that he sung, though not for me and the doctor, for his dog, the most favorite one of them all. That dog was the first one that he had so it was special to him, mainly because he received it from his late parents; they died when he was very young. One of them had died instantly of overexertion and he didn't notice it, until it was too late. (It is not aware how the other parent died.) The singing became louder and louder. He began to cry and then he said a prayer over the dog's body.

That was the last time that the small community of Deathville was ever heard of. Even in history books that locale is not mentioned. There is no trace that anything ever existed where the town supposedly was. Not even a splinter of wood could be found there from the old, damp, wooden houses. It's like it never existed. But if the town never existed, then I never existed either. It may have been all in my mind. [Since I never existed it couldn't have been all in my mind. If it wasn't from my mind, then from whose mind?]

[Author's Note: Thank you to my English teacher that assisted in the editing of the original story. Thank you Edgar Allan Poe for

The Lover's Death

the inspiration and insight. I have made slight grammatical changes while attempting to keep the same intent.]

around 7 February 1996

Volume 2: The Middle Years:
1998 — 2004

That Which is Within (Original)

"Hello? Mama? ... Mama?"

Jon-Jon held his breath and wished and strained to hear his mother's voice float through the wires and into his ear.

"Mama?"

And the only reply was his word's cold, dead echo off the mouthpiece and back onto his face.

Jon-Jon dropped the receiver and watched as it swung crazily; twice striking the glass walls of the phone booth before hanging like some odd, black bug.

He shook his head and sighed.

"Mama's not in there," said Jon-Jon. Then he shuffled down the empty street toward the next pay phone.

As he passed Mr. Denny's drug store, a movement through the plate glass yanked a dry scream from his throat. Jon-Jon cringed, whimpering, against the brick front of the building. (We [I] start after this.)

He heard a faint, voice, slow and purposeful from behind, however he could not discern whether it was a female or male.

Jon-Jon turned around slowly to see no one, not a soul. No trace of anyone being there, no disturbance in the wind, not even a fleeing shadow. Jon-Jon wondered what that voice could have been, was it even a voice? Or was he just hearing things, wishing that it was the comforting voice of his dear mother whom he had not seen or heard from in over three years. He did not know what to do.

Suddenly, a loud cracking sound came from the plate glass now to the left of Jon-Jon. Jon-Jon chose not to turn around too quickly so as not to immediately face the possible imminent terror that was waiting to pounce upon his hot, sweaty, yet chilled flesh. In his mind, he knew that he must do something. But, what thought should he choice, he had a myriad of ideas racing around in his head like cars on a racetrack. He was faintly aware of what was pending and what his next move, if he was that lucky, was to be. Jon-Jon pulled himself together, for he felt like the remains of a shattered fine vase that could not be discerned as once being whole, majestic and beautiful, and spoke some words, barely audible to himself.

"Whooo gooooes tttttthere?"

Jon-Jon could not fathom what he had mustered the strength, as a child raising up from falling flat on the floor, to say to the distant and cold stranger behind him. Jon-Jon smelt a musty, stale odor coming from the open area coming out of Mr. Denny's store. He felt the freezing air shift and return just as it had flowed out towards him, in a deliberate and slothlike pace. Once again, Jon-Jon behested that the life form behind him announce himself or herself. This time his voice was carried a

That Which is Within (Original)

little farther, and he actually heard himself speak.

"Whoo gooes tthere?"

    Jon-Jon's impatient and addled self could not wait any longer, like a child longing to open up presents on Christmas morning for the first time, and so he twisted his upper extremity so as to peek out with one eye to the southeast of his current position. Jon-Jon's left eye was twitching nervously as it made a calculated and deliberate look hastily towards the area behind him. His left eye blinked exasperatedly before he could turn his upper extremities around to face what was to the back of him. Jon-Jon knew that he had to garner the courage to do what he must, he had to see for himself what was behind him. At that very moment, he wished that he had the sensibility and the consciousness to call upon the eagles in the sky to use their magnificent sight to view what was behind him. Yet, he knew he could not that at this time.

    I spoke to Jon-Jon through his third-being, the true essence of him locked away, as if locked up in a damp, cold, dark dungeon waiting for the dismemberment of my already famished body during the times of the Spanish Inquisition, and told him that I was there with him at all times and the banal eyesore behind him would cause him no pain or discomfort that he would immediately experience. So as not to worry, I kicked Jon-Jon from the inside out to urge him to banish his reservations and look for himself. Jon-Jon knew I was right and that it was either now or never.

    During this time of Jon-Jon's simplistic, however very

complex reflections and deep contemplation, the spiritual manifestation behind him ceased to move or speak, only waiting for the moment when the southeasterly winds' chilling currents would stop blowing in his/her direction.

Jon-Jon felt the powerful kick, which thrust him a few feet in front of him from where he was standing and flat on his front side. Jon-Jon completely lifted himself off the ground and walked back to where he had stood just a few moments earlier. Jon-Jon saw nothing, except the brick side of the drug store and the plate glass. The glass had not been broken. Jon-Jon looked at the reflection in the mirror and it revealed to him his greatest horror, he was dead.

[Author's Note: This is the original short story (the revised story follows). It was written for a short story contest at *The Tennessean*, a Nashville, Tennessee newspaper, in 2000. The first part is what the person generating the story wrote to begin us and then we were to finish the story.]

Untitled: That Which is Within (Revised)

Sometime ago the story of Alrikien Sosquatoan Pableox Trumtkin was told to me as a child. I do not remember any more details other than what I am writing here. I do know that he served his purpose, as I must do the same. I have never met him, but I have felt his spirit graze by me on certain occasions when I am truly free and am at peace with myself and the whole universe around me and within me. I wish that he could understand what I now understand. I don't know if he ever will, I don't want him to think that I am trying to take too much credit for his life or his story, so I'll go ahead and tell his story.

Alrikien heard a faint voice, slow and purposeful from behind, however he could not discern whether the body behind the voice was female or male. Alrikien turned around slowly to see no one, not a soul. No trace of anyone being there, no disturbance in the wind, not even a fleeing shadow. He wondered what that voice could have been, was it even a voice? Or was he just hearing things, wishing that he had heard the comforting voice of his dear mother whom he had not seen or heard from in over three millennia. He did not know what to do. At that point in time Alrikien so badly wanted to reach out and hold someone, but of course, he knew that there was no one to hold on to, not even himself.

Suddenly, a loud cracking sound came from the plate glass now to the left of Alrikien. He chose not to turn around too quickly so as not to immediately face the possible imminent terror that was waiting to pounce upon his hot, sweaty, yet chilled flesh. In his mind, he knew that he must do something.

Untitled: That Which is Within (Revised)

But, what thought should he choose, he had a myriad of ideas racing around in his head like cars on a racetrack. He was faintly aware of what was pending and what his next move, if he was that lucky, was to be. Alrikien pulled himself together, for he felt like the remains of a shattered fine vase that could not be discerned as once being whole, majestic and beautiful, and spoke some words, barely audible to himself.

"Whooo gooooes tttttthere?"

Alrikien could not fathom what he had mustered the strength, as a child raising up from falling flat on the floor, to say to the distant and cold stranger behind him. Alrikien smelt a musty, stale odor coming from the open area coming out of Baba Crastamanition's local global food store. Alrikien felt the freezing air shift and return just as it had flowed out towards him, in a deliberate and slothlike pace. Once again, he behested that the Life Form behind him announces himself or herself. This time his voice was carried a little farther, and he actually heard himself speak.

"Whoo gooes tthere?!"

Alrikien's impatient and addled self could not wait any longer, like a child longing to open up presents on Christmas morning for the first time, and so he twisted his upper extremity so as to peek out with one eye to the southeast of his current position. Alrikien's left eye was twitching nervously as it made a calculated and deliberate look hastily towards the area behind him. His left eye blinked exasperatedly before he could turn his

Untitled: That Which is Within (Revised)

upper extremities around to face what was to the back of him. Alrikien knew that he had to garner the courage to do what he must; he had to see for himself what was behind him. At that very moment, he wished that he had the sensibility and the consciousness to call upon the eagles in the sky to use their magnificent sight to view, for him, what was behind him. Yet, he knew he could not do that at this time.

    I spoke to Alrikien through his Third-being, the True Essence of him locked away, as if trapped in a damp, cold, dark dungeon waiting for the dismemberment of my already famished body during the times of the Spanish Inquisition, and told him that I was there with him at all times and the banal eyesore behind him would not cause him pain or discomfort that he would immediately experience. So as not to worry, I kicked Alrikien from the inside out to urge him to banish his reservations and look for himself. Alrikien knew I was right and that it was either now or never. But, how could he, look behind him, he had not looked in that direction since he saw his mother abducted some time ago. Alrikien remembered screaming and calling out to his mother asking her to free herself, but she was too far away to hear his childish yelping for his very own mother. Since that time, he had not the reservoir of ambitious courage to look behind him and not see his mother there waiting with open arms and a smile that could light up the world. (Not much is known about his mother.)

    During this time of Alrikien's simplistic, however very complex reflection and deep contemplation, the spiritual manifestation behind him ceased to move or speak, only waiting for the moment when the southeasterly winds' chilling currents

Untitled: That Which is Within (Revised)

would stop blowing in his/her direction.

    Alrikien felt the powerful kick, which thrust him a few feet in front of his standing position and flat on his front side. Alrikien completely lifted himself off the ground and walked back to where he had stood just a few moments earlier. Alrikien saw nothing, except the brick side of the global food store and the plate glass. The glass had not been broken. Alrikien looked at the reflection in the mirror and it revealed to him his greatest horror, he was dead.

[Author's Note: The author believes that this short narrative was revised sometime in 2000 or 2001.]

Untitled: Speakable contemplations about Detroit experiential

Wit da absence of *Union Station* as tha ultimate "Beacon of hope" in an economically determinant sensitivity
    there came the *possibilities* that anything is possible when energies of the totality of our
        existence (energies, living, dead, yet to be born, in
        transit, spirits) seek a new definition of laughter
This laughter is none other a *spiritualawakening* which we don't create 'cause we are the created
¿Why does the *splashing of cold water* by a new found friend-relative (all our relations) feel so ecstatically dyNamite?
    The *white deer* call out our names as our closest relatives seeking a new way to enjoy the bounties of a laughing hyena parking outside in a green, yellow, Or$_A$nge, purple, polylectic looking *dots* that speaks of a new language of comedy
        Why comedy?
We never know why immediately in a chaotic and psychically hypnotic tone
    simple as complex thermodynamic interactions of 15th dimensional rotations in an avocado sphere
a bundle of J$_O$y perhaps?
        The *free-flowing/growing grass* and ghettonic palms create an atMustphere for
    life to commence in disguise
The *similar energies* emerged Sunday and continue to blossom as the dew sats on da baby boom of the African violet awakening from the *transformation of a house*
    The *sweat from the hard work* happens to be the dou

Untitled: Speakable contemplations ...

     falling like a torrential downpour of
     electromagnetic energy fields apon the above-
     mentioned family members
¿What's in a name? ¿What's in a name?
P
 e
  r   S
   h
    a   I
     p   T
    s   H
confused statement of individualized harmonies beating in one order of a mangled neck ripped apart by a carnivorous pack of unknown walking objects, but held together by the dis-ease state of the mucous-saliva entrode. The tree asks who we are and why we are here?

The American Revolution: Pages from a Negro Worker's Notebook
James Boggs

Racism and the Class Struggle: Further Pages from a Black Worker's Notebook
James Boggs

Conversations in Maine: Exploring Our Nation's Future
James and Grace Lee Boggs, Freddy and Lyman Paine

Living for Change: An Autobiography
Grace Lee Boggs

Untitled: Speakable contemplations ...

19 July 2001

Untitled: Poesía en a different tunor

Why?
Who?
When?
How ...?
What tha...?

What is this too curious, strange being asking now: Let me see,
    Is it this

What is the purpose of Life as we know it and do not know it?
¿Why are there not any straigHt lines in the Natural realm of the Universal cosmology [in particular the Earth – Mother]??
¿¿Who are you? ☺
When will we realize that WE MUST Change? But, how? And for what reason? Why can't things remain the SaMe?
How are you ...
        today?
this morning?
    this evening?
that afternoon?
                tonight?
Eating?
... Sleeping?
        Feeling? But, how do you feel? Do you really THINK you can feel emotIOns? [**That's ludicrous hogwash I tell ya!!** W...ell I do believe and *ThiNK* We do feel emotiOnS and so much More too!! ☺ }

Untitled: Poesía en a different tunor

¡¿When, I say... when, are YOU going to start thinking ... asking questions of Me, YOU, and of Life (thus all others]?

Or is it This Here!!:

How do you do?

    How do you do?

I asked you a question, so why are you asking me the same one in return, as a response?

    An answer was my response.

Say what?

    We mistake answers as only being statements, yet a question is also an answer. What is your perspective?

    That still does not make sense.

    Sense in what way? You must learn (relearn) to have your own line of questioning, thoughts, imagination, Creativity, problems, advice, SOLUTIONS ☺, interpretation, introspection, fallacies, peace, love, happiness, and so on. You must make the choice of your Fate and Destiny. What do you think, feel, taste, imagine, hear, see, experience (have the "*capacity* to experience" – so said the Buddha.} What is your point? What is my point? Are you right or wrong or neither? Am I right or wrong or neither? Are we both right or wrong or neither? What is Reality? [What

Untitled: Poesía en a different tunor

we see, hear, feel, and experience through our limited sensibility of senses?) What about what we can't yet understand, interpret, control, manipulate, steal, exploit, make war with and against, hear, feel, and experience? Is not this planet greater than you (what limited experience and imagination that you have)? What makes you exist? Me? This world? This dimension? This time, place, space? This realm? This thought, question, ideal, action? Why would one want to know ALL and destroy the Beauty of where we came from, aLL of US? Is there a ThEm? Do not questions beckon a call for more questions to trickle down or up or across or diagonally – depending on your perspective? Don't all beings exist? Thus we ALL have consciousness — whether you or I or someone else believes it or not.

Hold on, wait a minute!!☺ What's up with all these questions? I only asked you {how you were doing?]

And this Life Form would go on ... and ... on like this in each of the conversations, each and every day. I don't know why he can't answer a simple question without asking one in return. Why is that soooo hard?

     I am called the *QUestIoner* – Is not the way to the Truth [Realness, Essence, Vital Force, (Qi {Chi} – China, Ki – Japan, prana – India, pneuma – Greece, spiritus – Roman [Latin], ruakh – Hebrew), intrinsic energy, Life Force, internal power, Higher Being(s), Spirit/Soul, Ultimate Reality, Third Eye, Life] through peering at each level – starting at the surface or tip and scratching through to the core by asking questions? Is this not the way to "unmuddy the waters" so that they are pristine, clean, bright, beautiful, and clear? ¿Don't questions – thus the act or inact of listening, being quiet, thinking, imagining, creating, questioning – clear up fogginess of the mind? I do not ask aLL the questions, as I do not, nor wish to know them all. We aLL MUST ask questions – ALL of us if we are to transform. What is your purpose in Life – what are you going to imagine, QUESTion, believe, think, create, Be?

Thank-you *A Tai Chi Glossary* by Steve Brown and Larry Y. Brown, the Buddha, and Life.

Are not all beings people of some form or another? ¿Are not human beings ANIMals?? ☺

Thank-you Baba, my father.
¿¡questION!! ☺ Is there an othER?

"Then said a teacher, Speak to us of teaching.

"And he said:

"No man can reveal to you aught but that which already lies half asleep in the dawning of your knowledge.

"The teacher who walks in the shadow of the temple, among his

followers, gives not of his wisdom but rather of his faith and his lovingness.

"If he is indeed wise he does not bid you enter the house of his wisdom, but rather leads you to the threshold of your own mind. ..."

The Prophet
Khalil Gibran

Quoted in *To Educate With Love* by Dr. Herbert (Herb) M. Greenberg

[Author's Note: The author is using Khalil Gibran's 1923 book, *The Prophet*, published by Alfred A. Knopf as the copywritten source for the quote above. The author chose this quote because it exemplifies the essence of *the Questioner*. *the Questioner* asks that we use questions to guide us in our own understanding of Reality rather than relying on someone else. This idea is described in the quote above.]

31 July 2002 & 12 and 18 February 2014

Untitled: Questioning the War Against the People of Iraq

A history lesson. The U.S. is once again overtly going to war against the Iraqi people and is overtly trying to assassinate President Saddam Hussein, though we have tried to assassinate him covertly before and have supported him over the years.

Why did/do we support President Saddam Hussein?
Why are we at war with the people there again?
How many bombs have been dropped since 1989/1990?
How long have the airstrikes against Iraq continued, since 1989, 1990, 1991, 1998, or some other time?
Are there that many military targets or are we targeting civilians ("soft" targets) too?
Did the Reagan/Bush administration oppose congressional efforts to impose economic sanctions against Iraq in the 1980s? If so, why?
Did the Bush administration allow Iraq to invade Kuwait and then go to war for that same reason? If so, why?

Were/are President Saddam Hussein and former President/CIA Director George Herbert Walker Bush involved in "business" dealings?
Did the U.S. arm BOTH Iran and Iraq at the same time? If so, why?
Was the United Nations Special Commission (UNSCOM) used by the U.S. "intelligence" apparatus to spy on President Hussein of Iraq? If so, why?
Is the bombing and occupation of Iraq illegal, violating international law and the Constitution of the United States of

America?
How many people have been killed in Iraq because of the sanctions and/or the continuous bombings?
Haven't we learned anything from history?

Mr. Irucka Embry
Lexington, Kentucky

Printed in the *Lexington Herald-Leader* on Saturday, 03 August 2002 with other letters to the editor under the collective title of "U.S. Targeting Iraq."

[Author's Note: The author did not transfer his copyright over to the newspaper so he retains his rights.]

Untitled: Inter- or In- dependence of People

"You see these – they are MY BreasTs – NOt Yours!!? OKay?! ¿¿Do YoU see this vagina?! This is MY vagina also!! As well this on my backside is my butt – You UnderStand – MINE!? I'm tired of womyn being objectified in videos, in/on commercials, in magazines, and just in society …"

    Excuse me *BabY* – but in our society everyone is an object – a consumer robot and an object of consumption and objectification – that also applies to all ASpeCts of our Life in this society too. I understand where you're coming…

"in general is what I would have said before you rudely interrupted ME. So you don't and can't understand where I'm coming from – since you don't see that Men are always trying to dominate, manipulate, and be controlling – hence your interrupting ME! If you knew ME, you wouldn't claim that my body parts are YouRs – they are MinE. My parts are equally important in the WhoLe concept of MY Body. ☺ Though you only want parts of ME and not all of ME for some reason. This is MY body – I love myself, thus I am declaring MY <u>INDEPEND</u>ence from ALL men – including You – because We as WomYn are standing up and against male chauvinism/sexism, jealousy, violence, anger, exploitation, control, manipulation, technology, science, mode of thinking, lack of emotion/feeling, and respect/understanding of US – womyn!! ☺☹ We are reclaiming our *True* selves – womyn and not women – again – not <u>WOM</u>en and not wom<u>AN</u>. ¡¡¡So C-ya!!"

Untitled: Inter- or In- dependence of ...

OK – I understand your concern – I think.
So you will open doors for yourself now...
Pull out your own chair
Protect yourself
Pay for your own dinner/breakfast/lunch/snacks, bills, car notes, and so on
If you still *LiKe* MEN – US – *Will* you aPProach US and tell US that
You are interested?
Give your Self a massage and back rub
Ask Your Fellow *WoMYN* ☺ (yeah right - ¡Ha! Ha!! ☺] for help, assistance, support in solving YouR problems; giving you advice; cheering You Up; protecting You; helping you get unscared or Unfrightened and deal with YOuR feaRs; in fixing your car or sink or toilet or cutting your grass (Why does grass need to be cut anyways??!☺} or repairing other items in your residence; and let us not forget being your financial advisor/supporter, friend, confidant, teacher, and overall [re]usable toy for your eVery BecKoning call and whim. Or Will You DO that for Yourself?
{That'll be the day I tell ya]
When have you **ever** BeeN all that to ME or any other one of US?
Will you ever?
I said my Vagina, BreasTs, and butt because we were connected –
I thought – no OffensE to you or to your sensibilities.
Just as you say MY peNis – Ya Dig!? ☺
¿A partnership is 50/50 – isn't it?
We share ourselves – WhoLE and complete – with each other.
I was/am? your
     SouLmate
And You were/are? mine.

Untitled: Inter- or In- dependence of ...

I overheard a conversation between 2 parts of the WhoLe connection. Why were they angry? What is it that they see in each other that makes them so? Thus, what do they see in the MirroR? Why do they not fully appreciate themselves: (their gifts/talents, weaknesses, strengths] or respect or love or understand themselves fully? Why is it that we do not truLy understand OuR anger or happiness? Both of them are each good and evil and in-between, masculine and feminine, yin and yang and in-between, & interdePendenT. How can anyone be IndepenDent? How can any being be only dependent? Are we not ALl *inter*dependent? So there are not independent womyn or men. How can we appreciate, love, understand, respect, feel, hate, disrespect, misunderstand, unappreciate someone else until we can do so to ourselves? Each of Us has lightness and darkness – we should not dismiss either or destroy either. We should seek to embrace and appreciate both – as they each are a part of the WHoLe of each of us. I am neither good nor evil – I am good and evil and in-between good and evil – as we aLL are. I am known as the *QUESTioner*. Are not all humans born out of the union of the mother and father? So there is no true individual. ☺ Don't we aLL live on this planet together? Should not all people strive to be chivalrous to each other and to themselves? What is a partnership? A partner? A relationship? A friend? An enemy? Shouldn't we start with ourselves first? Why should we refLect on any idea or ideal or thought or person or action or inactIon? ☺ What does it truly mean to be alive and/or awake on this plane of existence? What about dead and/or asleep? Why are any of us here? Why are you here? Is there an US versus Them? Not if we are all connected, related, and ultimately interconnected and interrelated. Is there any separation? Is not that an act or

Untitled: Inter- or In- dependence of ...

thought or idea or inact of connecting oneself to a separate entity? Should not we ALL be responsible and accountable to ALL LiFe? Aren't we all a part of Nature/the "Web of Life"/the Whole? Should not we strive to liberate everyone and remember responsibility & accountability in this process and afterwards? Why not search for the Root/Source of your very existence and also your problems -? ¡¡Find Yourself! ☺

Thank-YOU to aLL of those who have given me the path to find my own answers and extend my own learning by lighting the path for me.

What is MINE? What is YouRS? What is OURS? ☺

4 August 2002

Untitled: Peace and not the "War on Terrorism" after 11 September 2001

Since the continuum of 11 September 2001 had effects worldwide, then why is it that not everyone in the world agrees with the current "War on Terrorism?"

In a sense, a continuation of the other wars that the US has been involved in — against people of color, socialists/communists, agrarian/land reformers, impoverished/poor people, and/or others that would stifle the profits of US corporations or resist US rule.

Is it because people are not satisfied with the evidence, or lack of evidence, presented by the current administration and our counterparts in the United Kingdom?

No more war, war will not solve the problems, only make things worse. We need the truth and the whole truth, not a piece of the truth. To truly honor those that died on that day and from the "War on Terrorism," the whole truth must be known and restorative justice must be the way to go, not retributive justice (vengeance). Ask questions of yourself and of the "official story line". Think and imagine a better world that works for all of us, not just some of us. Peace, the complete truth, and restorative justice are the answers, not war. "With great freedom comes great responsibility."

Irucka Ajani Embry is interested in continuing the search for the elusive Truth.

Printed in *The Daily Beacon* on Wednesday, 11 September 2002 with other letters to the editor under the collective title of "Student 9/11 Letters."

[Author's Note: The author did not transfer his copyright over to the newspaper so he retains his rights.]

Familial Vibrations

    It's that time of year again
Say what?
        LOVE, happiness, good home cooked { ☺ } [or store bought] food
        Insect bites, sneezing, wheezing, allergies, hay fever, injuries
Children laughing, smiling, crying, throwing rocks at each other
Bragging, climbing trees, running freely
        Sounds/sights of wild turkeys, deer, snakes, scorpions, coyotes, STARS
        Time for enjoying the LAND that our fore parents left for future generations to
Keep within the family as they worked so hard on the land for many years and worked hard to achieve their freedom from chattel enslavement
        Waking up early in the morning and feeling the early morning dew on the bottoms of bare feet while examining the dense fog that hasn't left yet
        Listening to the quietness, no longer in the air of the hustle and bustle of the city life – running here and there, deadlines, time checks, no time for family and friends
    Just work
Late nights talking and playing cards, walking and scaring each other, free-styling/rapping
    Late night hunger attacks
        Early morning wake up calls to clean chairs, move chairs, clean the H M Shelter, pitch tents/take down tents, rake leaves, take out the garbage, put up the sign, work on tin roofs in the

intense heat and under the bright sunlight, paint something --
anything

    Trips to R C Lane, where a portion of the Underground Railroad remains
    Reunion T-shirts, hayrides, games (Spades, Bid Whist, softball, football, soccer – world football, croquet, volleyball, Hand De Over), family histories/stories, meetings, fellowshipping, names, visitors, deaths, births, marriages, achievements, newsletters
    Reconnecting with each other and learnin' how we livin' nowadays
    Our mutual past comes alive when listening to stories of the old days before electricity at the "BIG HOUSE" and the days of raising animals and harvesting crops

Let's not forget trips to the stores (Wal-Mart) and to the hotels to escape the blistering heat
    Let us celebrate and enjoy the time that we have been blessed to share together with each other
    Let us remember that the future of M A (the family, the land, the legacy of history) affects ALL of us and the future generations should be included in such decisions and discussions
Let us fill our hearts up with love and joy and laughter throughout the weekend and remember the purpose of coming together with other family members

While down on tha farm, feel the love vibrating through the air and recognize that we are surely blessed to be a part of a large, loving, giving family with so much to look forward to in the future

Familial Vibrations

    Our good-byes last a Lifetime as we wish to hold on to the satisfaction of a time well spent enjoying each other's company

    My family is more than just a word that can be used so loosely and meaninglessly
        To me, my FAMILY is more than just blood relatives {my great-granddaddy H L M used to say "there's always room for one more"} brought together for family events throughout the year
    We are much more than that

\# 18 – 25 August 2003

Untitled: Questioning in tha Dream World

In a time devoid of space, width, length, height, depth, and other fantasmal human delusions of dimensional sensitivities there existed ... ☺

beings with form and some without consciousness. However, who can judge others without prior understanding?

Allow me to return to this depiction:

I visited this land of my own mental imagination or hallucination (as my mental health provider informed me after my lengthy visit to this land). Though I believe that this journey resulted out of deep meditation and an attempt to transcend my own unaware physical limits.

Here (where I came from), as a Life Form cemented in a form of a human being - MaLe -- I was direlected into a certain position with a distinct method of perceiving what I believed to be the Universes around me. I did not feel. Feel? What does such a word truly mean? Can any single word truly capture the experiential inclinations of the plane of existence we occupied?

I was emotionally empty. Spiritually bankrupt. Though mentally/intellectually able and stable. Physically could have been better as well. Psychically inept (as I only used five of my senses and none to their fullest octaves) and instinctually defunct.

Simply put, I was the product of an overly complex,

materialistic, chauvinistic/patriarchal, technological (developed & overdependent), rational, objective, falsely "scientific," violent, disconcerned & disconnected, religious (though lacking true Religion -- Spirituality), and unhealthy societal mind-set. Many of us were too blind to see that we moved too fast and had failed as a whole in all aspects. But, really, who was I to complain or speak about a system that I willfully participated in the dysfunctional activities of. Furthermore I have my own problems to speak about, though I won't disrupt the reader with that now.

As you (an audience member of the instruction of this piece) may be able to picture for yourself that the realm I came from was worth escaping. I tired of being a selfish, individualistic, rude, egotistical, chauvinistic fleshly male animal of the human variety. I wanted to grow in a limitless fashion and transform myself. I wanted to change how I functioned in ALL relationships and how I, as a product of a cruel and inhumane society, performed my proper role. It seemed that the female-male, female-female, and male-male interactions needed to be altered for a positive outlook. But, how? And why? Was I simply just delusional, crazy, strange, not "normal," or weird?

Was I a typical or atypical male? Who was I trying to fool? I was no better than anyone else. If anything I was worse and worthless.

I attempted to read various books on the healthful benefits of meditation and various techniques to try out to possibly reach a higher level of consciousness (Enlightenment). As well I wanted to find HOPE & the source of my existence and happiness so as to have reason to remain in this physical,

Untitled: Questioning in tha Dream ...

geometric shape on a continued basis. I had to try. What else should I have done? I was a failure and a wreck due to intense trauma and drama in result to my own weaknesses. I admit my faults and transgressions. Although my ego interferes when others approach me with such negativities. Oh well.

I traveled to a timeless locale with little so-called "developed" impact and interference. In the midst of the elegant microorganisms, plants, animals (non-humans), spirits, winds, and energies. Sitting down with my back and legs in a correct postural position. Bare feet. Legs, back, and stomach too. Wind-blowing through my hair and singing softly to my open, ready to listen ears. Covered my groin area with biodynamically grown industrial hemp cloths. The music of the world around me was music to my enchantable ears.

##

However, I was still not quite ready yet. I was not quiet. I was impatient with a myriad of mental images [thoughts} chasing each other around in my head. Born into an epoch in a society that does not value quiet reflection, listening to Self or others, it was no surprise to those with me why I was becoming agitated. We see those that wish to listen and be quiet fully as outside of the "normal" spectrum of human existence. Yet, who made them or any of us the judge of others? At the same time I knew that I had to transcend any limitations or boundaries placed on myself by others or even my own Self if I was to truly follow through in that which I sought.

Even with the underpinnings of addlings in my full body, I

had enough focus and concentration to keep my physical body still, even if not my Mind yet. Butterflies and ants showed their appreciation for my company by landing on my knees and crawling over my cellular outer structure (epidermal skin) as if I was a natural part of the scenic ecosystem. Or at least not regarded as an "enemy" or a "threat." I can not say the same, sadly, for my counterparts in the human world (as if we live in total separation and isolation from all other beings -- for those that think that we do, I'm sorry to hear that and I hope that you see that we are an intricate web interconnected and integrated with all others in the Total Web of Life). There, we place the title of "Enemy" (Grand isn't it??) on other people quickly for any real or imagined, slight or monumental, accidental or purposeful transgression against ourselves. Many times it can be traced back to pride or other inconsistencies of an ego overdeveloped and working in competition against an underdeveloped heart and spirit.

With me generalizing about others in that realm, some reading ~~my~~ Our story, may feel that the one spoken of here feels too righteous and perfect to claim the problems faced and dealt with on a constant basis. I'll only ask that you revisit the earlier part of this tale to see a different picture, hopefully.

For me, I started out with hatred and pain. In psychoanalytical terms, I had a sort of inferiority -- superiority combined complex. I felt that I was both better than and worse than others around me. This grew into a sort of pseudo-intellectualism and overall problems relating to others whom I did not feel were on my mental level. Let us not forget that this affected my ability to adequately listen to others (opinions, advice, experience, teachings, you name it). I don't want to feel that way. I am equal, not worth more or worth less. In my higher conscious Self, I see that and genuinely approach that ideal. My fault in that manner lies in the realm where the bloated ego reigns supreme or is at least treated accordingly.

To make things worse, I had the off-the-wall notion that I was NOT in my 1st Lifetime, but somewheres beyond 2nd or 3rd. Unsure of the exact number of journeys of my Spirit in various physical forms. This was so because most around me could not or would not fathom such an inexcusable, silly, blasphemous, strange, and/or weird idea. It was against their belief system and therefore could not exist.

Did you try to understand their perspectives or just give up totally on them understanding YOU in totality?

To answer your question, Self -- both. It's just that after a while you (let me make an I-statement here); well I became tired of having my deepest thoughts and feelings dismissed as insignificant and false. Maybe my ego felt a little bruised that they were possibly right and I was wrong. After all, they were larger in numbers than eye. I could not argue or fight with them all. Acquiesce or face a Life of turmoil, doubting my own inner wisdom/Truth, tension, and/or other negative consequences that I could bare to live without. I tried both options. I felt both were unsuccessful at times. I could not continue lying to mySelf to simply please others. As well, I tired of feeling like I had committed a grave atrocity for believing that which I did.

Options. Suicide. Denial. Hatred. Destroy Self/most

Untitled: Questioning in tha Dream ...

human fodder -- mostly those in my unAwakened society. Keep my views silent. Emigrate to a far away land with other like-minded beings. Keep trying. Give up. Educate mySelf more -- enter Self through meditation, as I currently wanted to do. Say screw the world and anyone not in agreement with my viewpoint. Change myself. Reduce my ego factor. I don't know. I have more questions than answers about that whole aspect and my tired Life in general.

    Another splendid example of my self-loathing. Can't forget those mutual feelings for other robots (referred throughout as human beings, humans, or people -- mistakingly for the most part). How did I come into this being with so much prior knowledge and imagination? Why so much negativity? Why the thoughts of death -- suicide? Why the Self-hatred? What had I done previously? What baggage was I still holding on to? How did this affect those around me – close and not? Did I care? If not, why not? Did they care? Do they know? What did they know? What did they understand? What did they not? If I died at a young age, would it have mattered to anyone? I would have cared, even if I don't always feel that way about this Self. What is/are the purpose(s) of Life anyways?

    How could I have not seen how my actions, thoughts, feelings affected those that I supposedly cared about? I guess I didn't care for whatever reason. Scarred ego? Ego-trippin'? False pride? Feelings of worthlessness? Fear of others' opinions of me? Or fear that I may actually feel that I am worthwhile and worth living for? What did I have to fear? The future? That's right.

Untitled: Questioning in tha Dream ...

Some archaic view of saving the Earth, when you don't care enough to save your self. Funny, isn't it? Don't want to hear this Truth, do you? Close your ears. Cry if you wish to. Cleanse your soul. Free yourself. How can you help others if you can't first help yourself? You are disconnected indeed. Reunite yourselves. Become whole again.

In my view, you have possibly suffered a severe schism when entering the womb into the beginning cellular form. Head trauma at birth? Fear of karma for your past transgressions? Fear of facing such responsibility? Of loving yourself unconditionally and others? Of a brighter future? Of being happy and seen smiling or laughing? Of letting others possibly having the potential to get to know and understand you? What do you think? It's OK. Let your ego go. Let the tears flow. It does not make you any less or more of a person in my our eyes. I'm saying this for your own good only.

My own good!? That is what I've been told my whole life by so-called good-meaning people. By the way, what does that mean anyways? They are no better than I and me no better than they. Experience. That's the ticket. Or is it maturity? I don't know. Don't I possess those innate qualities too? Even if at different levels. Does what I think, believe, or imagine even matter? I am not perfect, though I attempt to strive for perfection -- at times. I do know that I do NOT possess those attributes, as I do not possess myself. Let alone a second of time or someone else. Time -- that most magnificent dimension that many have tried to possess, control, manipulate, imitate, comprehend, but really can't. Time is beyond us, yet within us. Time is everywhere and nowhere at the same time. When we don't exist anymore, time will still exist and persist. Thus, our distaste: **DEAD**lines, rush hour, minute or minute, "microwave" society, and other clues to our lack of understanding of time. Especially how time can and does affect us directly and indirectly.

    I did it. I turned a battle of wits and words with an inner-self into a thoughtful and polite discussion of time and place. How? I cooperated and did not compete. I attempted to listen and not merely hear. I wanted to understand and not simply react and judge, though I did at first. I wanted to eventually embrace and not Confront. Love not hate. Be truthful and real with mySelf. Take responsibility. Figure out why I am the way that I am. This is why I journeyed to this sacred place (though I feel that we are all sacred indeed). To find the person I could not find before. Because of a lack of searching? Or not knowing how to look? Who was I searching for that I could not locate?

    MySelf. ☺

###

    Question: If you could not find yourself, how did you exist? How did you know that you existed? What makes one exist or not exist? Is an answer a question or a muddled riddle? Or is a question in response, a question or an answer? How does one know? Can one figure oneSelf out or must one find oneself? What makes us who we are? Can Life be explained in solely scientific terminology? Or should it also include the convergence with spirituality? Are we mere "victims" of circumstance and various unrecognizable patterns of probabilities? Or are we affected by invisible (to the naked eyes), yet visible [to the Third

Eye} webs or energies of an omnipresence? Divine origination? Could it possibly be a mixture of both? Nah, couldn't be -- remember the separation or gulf between science and spirituality? Anyways, that was my question. Not necessarily to answer on my own or vicariously, but to cause some rumblings of neurons in an imaginative and thinking fashion.

    Some may have pegged ~~me~~ us as a "know-it-all," pompous, arrogant/conceited, superficially deep, abnormal, "scientific" (thus lacking false "religion"), unhappy, thuggish, nappy-good haired, overly cautious and predictable, boring, overly sensitive of Self - yet insensitive of others, contradictory, depressed, young, and immature mess of atoms, molecules, DNA, RNA, cellular structures located within a limited experiential male creature of the human animal species. Personally, I exist on various levels in this world of my extraneous presence, levels such as emotional, physical, spiritual, psychic, intellectual/mental, vibrational, energetic, and so on and so forth. So what does all of this truly mean? Either others have failed to recognize my aura, Essence, chi, ruakh, ki, True Spiritual Presence as they may have been cloudy at times or because they chose not to look beyond my distractive [purposeful) outer shell. Or is this my fault as I did not drain the moat or provide a bridge for people to cross over and to fully investigate the inside of my ethereal castle? Thus, why have I thwarted honest attempts to discern the question of "who really was I?" Was this an attempt to hide myself or because I felt that others may try and get too close to me if I let them near or inside me? Why was I hiding? Who was I hiding from? Did I know or care? Was I perfect? Did I believe others expected such perfection from a mistake? How could one know that which they could not access? That's including myself. Which chambers were I unwilling to open and why? Was my karma that malignant? If so, why? If not, then why had I led myself to believe that? Was I a "victim" of a caustic social order? Or was my Life my responsibility and thus my fault when I failed as I did on many occasions? Though is failure just success turned inside out? Or is it vice versa? You decide. No we'll decide. How does one, if one does or can, rise up above his or her circumstances and surrounding environmental influences? Why would one want to do so if one could? That is not necessary, is it?

    The cycles of question/answer question/statement question/thought question/imagination question/ continued in my convoluted head and exasperated my already fractured state. I was in need of opening up my heart -- Spirit -- and lessening my overdependence on the more analytic system of Self. The conceptual system of patterns and relationships was closer to my broken and damaged heart. Hurt by my own ill doings and not-doings to others around me (as well as to myself.]. I also ached of the lost ones due to my own personal problematic responses based more so on vengeance(?), than on the higher qualities that I wish to attain one day and move beyond. We are always changing, whether we know it or not. Changes are what prompts growth and vice versa and caused this entity to adapt/respond in a different light, even if only in theory up to this point and not in practice. How could anyone in their right mind love or respect a practicing heathen, a pagan after all, who has too much scientific/mathematical theoretical outlooks being pumped out of his cerebrum and dissipated through channels out of tha larynx. Either he is a "mad scientist" believer in evolutionary theories of creation or a follower of false modals of "religious" conception. Could he be who he says he is? – An ancient Spirit?

Not possible. Implausible. Impractical. False. Not theoretically possible.

Could he believe in an "us" versus "them" idea of Life conceived by good-willed Higher Beings? Could others really believe so? Was he brainwashed to think and imagine differently? Could he simply not see the invisible or visible evidence? Was he too limited by his so-called "scientific" bias? Was he trying to figure out instead of trying to find out? Who was to decide? Who could judge? Was he right, wrong, or neither? What did he *really* feel, think, believe, imagine, understand, have faith in, and so on? Did anyone ask or believe? Did anyone care? Did he care? Is this what he feared or thought that he feared? Did he really fear or just wish to avoid disappointment? How much of his self-wroth was determined by others? By his own recognition? Who is he? Did he know? Or was he searching? Did he realize that science and spirituality converged? If so, at what point in his Life? How did he know? Did he think he knew all of it or some of it? How did he approach the mysteries of the Divine Feminine/Masculine within him?

You (the reader) may ask if I am telling the tale of mySelf, though written by someone else. If so, then who is "he?" He is I and I am he. I am the subject of this his-story. I am like the writer, but not completely so. Even so, we are both One, and not the Same. Our collective journeys never crossed, yet we feel each other. A feeling that can not be described accurately nor analytically in reality. But, why those limits of your Life -- science?

Untitled: Questioning in tha Dream ...

Note: The following conversation includes various possible interpretations of the Christian (Judeo-Christian tradition) religion. I (as the writer/interpreter) and the subject of interest do not condemn Christians nor Christianity.

This interview was not done (completed) in the usual manner. He approached me in the Dream World and asked that I pen his memoirs and this is just and interview of some of his thoughts. Please recognize that certain aspects may be overly deep, scientific, castigating of Christianity, spiritual, shallow, contradictory, biased, and/or irrational.

Questioner {Q}: He who I hath sought (well actually I did not know of his existence -- he approached me}. How he knew I existed? I don't know.

Dream Thatcher (DT): That is how he described me. Go figure.

Q: Dream Thatcher, welcome to the Dream World. I have patiently awaited your return to this side.

DT: Dream Thatcher? Were you talking to me? That is not my name. How do you know me? Do you know me? What do you want?

Q: Listen to your heart and you'll know.

...

Untitled: Questioning in tha Dream ...

DT: I will cautiously attempt to do as you have asked of me. Thank-you for your confidence in me. I genuinely appreciate that. I'll purify myself with you in a sweat lodge as you've requested. ...

After many visits to the Dream World, the Questioner eventually asked me to interview him. It was not spoken, as our first conversations had been, through words. Though we still communicated, it was through extra-sensory perception (ESP). It was an amazing and exhilarating experience overall. I learned about myself as we continued on the journey through his sordid Life.

DT: Who are you? When were you born? How did you perish physically?

Q: Who am I?
Who are you?
Do any of us truly know? Can we? Should we? Does it matter? Don't we walk around without knowing? Do children know? Does it matter if one is emotionally or spiritually dead? Who determines what?

I classify or categorize myself as a being. A Life Form, if you will. Then as an animal. Next as a human being. Lastly as a male (a major portion of my Essence favoring the masculine rather than feminine characteristics). The name(s) I was/were originally and subsequently born with are not labels, but they are explainers of my existence. However, I am much more than that. Let's get beyond the superficial to the surreal. I can not give you my date of birth, as those in your time and place do not yet understand that they use a rather recent calendar system. It has not always been used and is not used all over the world now in your time either. They have a false sense of their temporal self. We viewed the concept of time in a different light altogether. Time was not to be controlled, manipulated, or fought over. Time, like all other aspects of the Universes, was sacred to us.

I perished physically at different temporal positions in the history of the Earth -- my Mother. The last time was in the lovely Inquisition.

DT: What do you think about your persecution?

Q: Hatred, fear, jealousy, misunderstanding, control, greed, indifference to wants and needs were the Inquisition's precursors. The Christian (Catholic) rulers used those negative feelings already in existence and directed the people to focus their common problems on the "enemy." The "enemy," of course, caused all of their problems and not themselves. The "enemies" were non-Christians, healers, scientists, heretics, blasphemers, free-thinkers, and others that pointed out the fallacy of the monarchy and our constant reliance on blaming scapegoats for all of our own problems. Our lack of personal/political responsibility and accountability of our religious "fanatic" leaders were other downfalls.

####

It has been my experience that this religion uses various methods of control and manipulation to get people to accept the status quo of inequality. No one is able to question authority or the reasons why the Gnostic Gospels are NOT included in *The Holy Bible* (Basic Instructions Before Leaving Earth). Those Gospels, as I understand, were written completely or mostly by women. Why were the Gnostic Gospels not included? Lack of space? Was the full Life of Jesus Christ written out completely in the New Testament? What did the 1st people to believe in God, as the present-day Christians do, call themselves? What language was the Bible originally written in? Why all the translations, omissions, deletions, and additions over the years? Let's not forget the changes in meanings too. Since Christians have persecuted people for hundreds or thousands of years, why do they feel that they are being attacked for no apparent reason? I do not and did not support those violent attacks, but a reckoning must come to discern the True history of the Christian faith in the world. Re-exploring the Holy Crusades, enslavement, colonialism, corporate globalization, capitalism/imperialism, the Inquisition, and other historical and current persecutions of the Earth's children under the guise of "civilizing" or "democratizing."

People are controlled to accept the belief that women are inferior and less than their male counterparts. This relegates women to a second-class citizenship whereas they may become accustomed to be treated with ill-contempt. Their male counterparts develop, on the other hand, a superiority complex of some sort and expect to be treated royally while ignoring women who should expect and want that. Let us also remember that children too are unheard as they are not important yet. This rift affects the psyche and over-all well-being of the feminine & masculine which must be balanced in order to have order & balance & harmony. If women were so repulsive & of less importance, why was the female body chosen as the portal from which all male & female children of the human species arrive into and exit from? From water to air. If both males & females view each other as sacred & worthwhile, then the complexes would be distended. As well, balance would be restored and each would respect & love themselves and each other. Though this cannot happen until it is acknowledged that we do not exist as separate entities. We are merely webs of relationships interwoven and intertwined in a larger, grander interlocking universal Web of Life. Our bodies are full of relationships between atoms & molecules, tissues & muscles, air & water. All of those components are made of empty space & energy. Thus this energy flow connects all of our energies to each other and to the energies around us.

We are always in a relationship to ourselves and to others. We **all** breathe the same air, drink the same water, and feel similar emotions and think similar thoughts as those that have come before us and those that are present and those that will come in the future after us. This is the Cycle of Life. We are not the beginning nor the ending. What we do affects all others.

Imagine a body of water. Throw a pebble in the body. Observe. Listen. Feel. The waves are circular and extend from the point of contact. How is the air affected? What about the further regions near the shores (banks)? Has the level of oxygen changed? How does that simple act alter the existing ecosystem and in turn the other interconnected ecosystems?

What do you hear? The wind? Birds? The water?

What do you feel? Changes in temperature? Movement of wind? Emotive changes? How do you view what you have just experienced?

Why did you feel that you **had** the right to perform such an act? Was it because the Earth is to be subdued to human interests? Was it because you do not view the water is sacred? That you came from water and that you are 70% water. Let us not forget that our Mother is also 70% water too. How can you forget to remember your connection to water? Your dependence on water's cleanliness and quality. As well, the beings that we consume also depend on water for their survival and in the process your survival as well.

As long as the Earth is irrelevant and Heaven (above and beyond the Earth) is revered and relevant, what I have said has no bearing on the minds of many people. I feel that all Life is sacred and worthy of respect as we all have consciousness. Science is slowly coming to this conclusion and maybe one day the general Christian religion will revisit its roots, those "lost" and those known, and rediscover the True Faith versus the watered-down, manipulated version presented as the Truth in this current day and age.

The Truth is always elusive to those who wish to evade it and deny its existence. Oh well. The Truth is that our emotions, thoughts, feelings, and actions not only affect us, but all others too. Remember that it was mentioned that the feminine & masculine exist together and cannot be separated. This is also true for our connection to all other beings in the physical realm. If we believe in that conception of Reality, then all beings deserve respect and reverence, as we also deserve and warrant the same.

Some within the Christian religion have contended that other beings, other animals, have to be respected as we respect other humans. All of this has not been a critique of Christians themselves, has much as it has been a critique of the religion of about 30% of globe today. Various scholars believe that the Judeo-Christian vantage point has brought forth the ecological crises due to the separation of people from the rest of Creation. What do you (the reader) think?

Reaching back to the idea of control and manipulation. The idea of having a hellish life to enjoy paradise in the afterlife in Heaven supports a status quo where a small worldwide group benefits materially (in extremity) as compared to most of the people in the world. Hence people will not question why the preacher, priest, minister, bishop, and so on are *filthy* rich and the other members of the church struggle day-to-day. This is accepted since happiness comes at the end of a tortured Life in which one is both torturer and toruree. Destroying the irrelevant Earth and rest of Christian and being forced to accept an unequal Reality. Women, children, and men stick to their roles. Those in the upper echelons of society continue to thrive and those at the latter end try to Live each day (in terms of basic needs). It is important to note that to be controlled and/or manipulated, one must accept it. The only way one can be constrained is if one allows it to happen.

I may be enslaved or constrained physically, but that's it. The rest of me is free and I will strive to free myself fully as well. As I realize that I can only be enslaved if I allow it to happen. This means taking responsibility for not only your actions, but for what also happens to you.

The other aspects of control deal with FEAR. One cannot question the authority of the priest, minister, bishop, or pope (God). One cannot question the various inequalities and contradictions. One must blindly accept, with no thinking allowed. This allowed the Catholic (Christian) King Ferdinand and Queen Isabella to continue their rule and conquest of what became known as the Americas. Their richness correlated with the expulsion of the Jews, the end of the Moorish rule, the conquests of Christopher Columbus, and the stagnant Life of people in Castille-Leon who could not rise up the social ladder due to their own lack of financial resources, while the King and Queen amassed much material wealth and enslaved Taínos (Arawaks). But, who was brave enough (of a high-enough social class) to question all of this? How did the heads of the Church benefit materially simultaneously? Does the same apply, even if only partially, to the set-up today? Ecological destruction, death, pillaging, raping, and enslaving followed the armies of the Church. Let us not forget "new, willing converts."

So, why does one accept all of this? Heaven -- that's right. Do reincarnation, soul travel, dream world(s), psychics, and so on exist? Does the Bible speak against them? Are they mentioned in the Bible? If people can live for over 500 years, why can't people's spirits return to a physical body? {Spirits exist in all beings, not just humans ya know.] Would God allow that? Have you (the reader) asked God that? Is the Bible totally complete and unaltered? If Jesus' soul returned to his physical, Earthly body, would God allow other souls to return to the Earthly realm as well? Do we know what is allowed and accepted by God? Is there only one way to speak to the Divinities, Creators, Gods/Goddesses? There are over 6000 languages, why is the Bible mostly spread and featured in one language -- English? Can both the Earth and Heaven be seen as being sacred? Did Jesus condemn the synagogues and temples? Can this be extended to churches as well? Is the objective to attend a church or to follow your heart and your connection with your view of the Higher Being(s)? Did Jesus preach/speak in a church? Did he preach about ending suffering and misery in the present Life? Did he speak of what we now call economic and social justice? So why don't others who believe in Jesus and "what he does," join in the global movement for justice? If God created the Earth and all Creation, why do we desecrate Her and all creation? Does that please God? Does that show appreciation or contempt for the work of God? I am not your (the reader) judge; I am only questioning authority in an attempt to unravel the Truth.

#####

So what exactly is the Truth? Is there only one or are there many Truths? Just different facets of the Collective Universal Truth(s)?

Looking back at religiously? If you participate in religious services, ceremonies, and such, do you know what the symbols, actions, spoken words, and so on mean? Do you understand them? How are they significant? What is the purpose? Do you care about the answers to this latest barrage of inquisitive questions? Does your Faith or lack of it allow you to question what you do or do not take part in? Were religions created by people for the explicit/implicit purposes of control, domination & manipulation? Are the various global religions fundamentally the same in the basic core tenets and beliefs? Thus, are we more similar than different? What is Spirituality? How does it differ from religion?

In the viewpoint that I have taken thus far, religion =ed Spirituality from the beginning of time. However, for some reason or another there was a catastrophic split between the two (once one). This is just one of the various splits that have taken place over time though. As well, the split from/of religion = Spirituality/science; splitting of Earth/Heaven/Universe; splintering of the body into various unconnected and disrelational, separate body parts, and various other transformative cleaves. What caused these to occur and how can we reconcile these differences and make ourselves and our perspectives of the Universe whole again? Does it really matter? I sincerely hope that you, the reader, understand that the many questions are posed for good reasons. If we do not Truthfully and accurately know whence we came, do we know where we are? Are we moving forwards or backwards? Evolving or devolving? Do we know where we are going? And more importantly, where we can go? That is by using our collective, "individualized"

Untitled: Questioning in tha Dream ...

potentials of Creative and Imaginative Energy to chart a different course or we very well could make ourselves EXTINCT. This is what we are facing and we must transform ourselves if we wish to survive. This will be a radical, full-scale Revolution as reformations only placate the symptoms and leave the interrelated problems intact. The Christian Reformations did not solve the central, root problems. It's possible that it like other false solutions to real problems caused more problems and hurt, than it alleviated signs of problems (symptoms).

I'll discuss my role in The Inquisition as survivor, not victim.

19 August 2003
27 August 2003
2 September 2003
27 September 2003
30 October 2003

Nightmarish vision

United
Stolen lands of
Aggression

No wrongs done here
Ignorance
Great "Liberator" or Great Liar
Happy consumers
Technologically over-dependent
Money is the answer
A false historical perspective
Rivers of blood and bones
Ecological destruction

7 September 2003

A tour of the Empire

American Dream

What comes to your mind?

US Nightmare. For me and for many others [not deluded by the false glamor and glitz of such a lie as a separate "America" excluded above and beyond the rest of the Western Hemisphere states), we believe that an American is anyone from a nation in the Western Hemisphere. Thus, the continents of North and South America.

Furthermore, when those robots of this enchanted place of extreme polarity of inequities speak of American, they mean a person of European descent who practices Christianity. In other words, a person racially classified as white or Caucasian. The whole "racial" thing is a topic in itself to be discussed in full one day. Did you know that the word "American" originally referred to the Native American peoples? That was until sometime after the War of 1812.

> Now that's enough of your socialist-communist, Marxist-Leninist critique of this great country that all people wish to emigrate and journey to. ... To see the roads paved with gold and the place where anyone's economic dreams can be made a reality in no time. What comes to your mind?

In my mind I see the first modern democracy.

The society built out of the ideals of the Renaissance, the Enlightenment, separation of Church & State and science & religion, and rationalism. Those great theories from Old Europe were put into practice in this nation-state, the greatest ever to exist. We even improved upon the Roman Republic and the Greek democracy. We know that God blesses everyone in this society because we are the best. This is the land of equal opportunity for everyone that works hard and doesn't complain about foolishness like discrimination based on skin color (racism), sex (sexism), sexual orientation (homophobia), age (ageism), disability (mental/emotional or physical), socio-economic status, and so on.

The American Dream is great because we take the promise of a great future due to the English language -- (the American version – which is better than the British version. Plus English is the best language ever. It's not our fault people can't speak it correctly.} -- with us all over the world via our multinational corporations and give-outs of aid to the rest of the world. We are what makes this world go 'round. Though we are not perfect, we are definitely close to it, as near as possible. People hate us because of our freedoms and because we won't let them in to benefit from our freedoms. It's not our fault that they messed up their countries, we tried to offer them assistance, but *they* didn't want help from a Western government. Such ignorant and backward fools. I know all of this because this is what I've always been told so it must be true. I wouldn't be lied to by my country – the greatest in the world – would I be?☹

A tour of the Empire

Thank-you for your **correctly**, wonderful dissertation. ☺ I really appreciated it. It's a great way to distance myself from that ... other response. And don't you start questioning the integrity of our nation, we wouldn't lie to you. We are the greatest. That is why we are so proud.

Um, excuse me!! Let me leave both of you with some thoughts on the US nightmare:

Bloody hands
    Remove and throw away the gloves
Recession
    Massive tax cuts for the already over-materially wealthy and further loopholes in off-shore banking account regulations

Disagreement with another country
    Forced assimilation (acculturation to be frank and exact) and
economic, social, political, and environmental warfare

    No need for diplomacy – our military stretches around the globe and there is
no one to restrain our illegal activities – either too scared of repercussions or complicit

Send people away to fight banker's wars
    Bring them back in HRPs (Human Remains Pouches)
    Cut benefits for veterans and their families

    If they complain of illness

Deny access to medical care
Deny medical information – vaccinations, experiments, biological/chemical/radiological toxins used

If they stand up for their rights
    Have them put down with their families in the nation's capitol
    Just don't report too much on it

If they stand up for peace and justice,
    Call them traitors
    Deny their accusations
    Say they're communist or socialist
    Once again put them down and others around them
    Give them great gov'ment positions to quiet their rage at being wronged and doing wrong
    Have other veterans and/or patriotic robots of this land march against those traitors and their supporters
    Discredit them in any way
    "Release the dogs" – CIA, FBI, ONI, DIA, MIA, ATF

National problem
    Blame it on the Mexicans, Muslims, Arabs, Blacks (African-Americans), homosexuals, and/or any other group that would make an easy scapegoat (read: target)
    Start a war, bomb a nation
        Anywhere,
        Somewhere
        Just do it

A tour of the Empire

Decrease in the national crime rate
    Build more prisons
    Why?
    Preparing for economist bust?
    Hire more police/corrections officers –
    Don't they have violent tendencies according to personality tests?
    Did someone say police brutality?

So what!! They're protecting our freedoms and serving us!!

International visitors to Atlanta, Georgia for '96 Olympics
    Ship the people out to other cities
    What people? – Homeless people
    Can't let the world know we're not a land of opportunity ("of milk and honey")

Undesirable populations
    Send them to the ghettos, reservations {first concentration camps), trailer parks, rural areas
    Send them to prison, to the military

Undesirable movements for positive social change
    Discredit them
    Assassinate characters
    Assassinate actual participants and others around them
    Miseducation
    Warfare (chemical, psychological, and economic)
    Infiltrate
    Quiet them

Destroy them
Just do it

Democracy or Republic
 Which one is it? Or is it something entirely different?
 Oligarchy (oiligarchy), aristocracy, meritocracy, plutocracy, and/or a mixture of those socio-economic systems

This is our history, present, and future until we do something about it.
Think, imagine a new way.

Acronyms of various US agencies

C.I.A. = the United States of America Central Intelligence Agency (formerly the Office of Strategic Services – OSS)

F.B.I. = Federal Bureau of Investigations

O.N.I. = Office of Naval Intelligence

D.I.A. = Defense Intelligence Agency

M.I.A. = Military Intelligence Agency

A.T.F. = Bureau of Alcohol, Tobacco, and Firearms

N.S.A. = National Security Agency

A tour of the Empire

N.R.O. = National Reconnaissance Office

F.E.M.A. = Federal Emergency Management Agency

Goon squad(s)

Military

Police

KKK

(neo)-Nazis

Organized crime (worldwide Mafias)

Trained and organized gangs and other groups

7 September 2003

Warfare for the Future

Genetic integrity lost
Eugenics
No questions, it's pure science
Exceptional myths
Technology – why the beef?
Insecticides
Concentration camps

White supremacy
Accept or be labeled "anti-science" or "anti-progress"
Rape and pillage the Earth
Food – what is it now?
Are you sterilized yet? You're an "undesirable."
Regulation by the promoters
Exactly what do you need to know?

7 September 2003

Attack of the ...

"Warfare for the new generation" constantly aired over the airwaves.
I must be one of the few hearing that.

Why you may ask?

'Cause there are not riots taking place all over this place now. If someone makes a comment about curtailing freedoms or how other people view us, then we get our "feathers ruffled" and speak up and out. However, when our "corporament" (corporations & gov'ment) declare genetic warfare against us, we jump up for glee and couldn't be happier.

>We're going to feed the world.
>End malnutrition and malnourishment.
>Decrease the use of agrichemicals.
>Increase the yield per acre.

All of this at what cost?

Loss of
>Biodiversity
>Genetic and overall ecological integrity
>Small-scale, family farms
>Knowing what we are putting into our bodies (if we ever knew under the age of industrial agriculture)

Are those promises worth it?

Attack of the ...

What if they fail? -- As they already have.

What are we going to do?
    Ask for less gov'ment regulation
    Boycott the corporations involved
    Educate yourself on the alternatives and practice those methods
    Buy food using those alternative means
    Ask for more gov'ment regulation
    Question the scientific basis of genetic engineering
    Demand ethics and accountability in science

What are *you* going to do?

7 September 2003

[Author's Note on 1 and 8 February 2014: The term "corporament" comes from the equation: corporation + government = "corporament" while recognizing that the corporation = government, i.e., the government institutions and corporations have the same source. I originally defined the term in an article, entitled "A personal look at our government," which was printed in *The Daily Beacon* as "Opinion: Our government can not be trusted" on Monday 26 August 2002. {Find the article at http://www.questionuniverse.com/oldway/columns.html.}

In the USA, the "corporament" exists as the:

military (defense/offense) + industrial + academic (schooling − at all levels – as prison) + "corporament" entertainment (Hollywood, media, advertising/consumerism/commercialization, propaganda /psychological warfare) + judicial (defense and prosecutorial lawyers, judges, law enforcement/police, prisons) + financial (banks, accounting firms) + religion + petrochemical/pharmaceutical (drugs, antibiotics, antibacterials, vaccines, pesticides – toxins to kill or put you at "dis-ease" and drugs to "treat" you) + imperial commu-soci-capitofasdemocracism system/society /economy/Western thinking = Military-industrial-academic-"corporament" entertainment-judicial-financial-religion-petrochemical/pharmaceutical complex.

Commu-soci-capitofasdemocracism is derived from communism, socialism, capitalism, fascism, democracy, and republic as these concepts all have the same root. The complex was originally defined in the aforementioned article, but it has been recently revised to reflect a new understanding of the complex's nature.

The complex was broken down further in an excerpt of a still "Untitled" song written by the Hip Hop artist Vibration Kunvorted off of his *What Do U Feel?* album {http://www.vibrationkunvorted.com}:

"We are all One / Awareness / of Infinite Consciousness / don't be fooled / or schooled / by the Illuminati – Global Elite – Higher Dimensional Negative Consciousness / imprinting their design / in tha vocal chords & symbolism / of da Intelligentsia, media personalities, journalists, scientists, designers, engineers, architects, intellectuals, medical personnel, social services (SS) workers, religionists, globalists, musicians, activists, politicians,

Attack of the ...

teachers, actors, leaders, executives, ad nauseum for centuries past / 'cause their rule is not going to last"

Basically, the US "corporament" is one head of the galactic/global elite body.]

Dreamin' anew

Dirty
Rotten
Egotistical
Absence of a true picture of reality outside our island prison/paradise
Machines

Anglo-Saxon
Murder
Excess
Regressive
Impulse
Cancerous
Are they people or robots inside human skin?
Now what are we going to do?

or

A new vision of people and our relationship to each other and to our Mother, the Earth

Now is the time to change ourselves first
Ecological thinking
Water is plentiful, pure, and FREE

War becomes unpopular and peace & justice rise in its absence
Ancient ideas blend with modern theories – Convergence

Dreamin' anew

You and I, we walk together with hope and vigor as we come together to create a new future

7 September 2003

Rumblings for the children

Simplicity
    Understanding
        Spirituality
            Take back our lives from our
masters/enslavers
                Act like we have a
common future
            Invigorate a new sense of
personal/political responsibility
        New vision of health & wellness

Hearts open-wide
        Opportunities for growth and reflection
            Purpose and prosperity
                Education in
sustainability

for

Artistic creativity
        Nature
            Older voices/visions join with newer
voices/visions
                Teach – about a new
way – in a new way
                    Healing
            Express creativity
        Reflections of a brighter future out of

Rumblings for the children

our commonly shared past

      Wake up
Open your mind
          Release the toxins (hatred & anger)
        Love
              Dream

Insight
      Share

Passion
      Observe
           Solve problems in better ways
              Security based on
respect, trust, honesty, & mutuality
            Inclusivity
      Balance in the Present
Laughter
      Earth Charter

7 September 2003

Fixability in a Brokable Fashionablement

                                        Bereaving over the loss
of that special someone
                          Responsible for my own actions
           Opportunity to see the relationship in a new light
Kissing no more

                                   Emotionally, spiritually,
physically, and mentally detached from the rest of the world
                                    No reason to hold back
the flood of saline tears

Hatred poisons my aura like a toxic venom
              Every day counts
                     Arguments no more
                               Rippin' apart the bonds
we once shared
                                            Take it
personal no more
                               Enjoy Life – you're not
Dead
                 Dance and Dream

8 September 2003

Reflections on that which did not exist

Lies
        Outside interference [for better or worse}
            Violence & vengeance
                Egos colliding

              Love, infatuation,
and/or hormones (depending on Ur perspective]
           Opportunity for growth, reflection, &
personal change
      Selfishness
Try again

Just what is

        O
L   V
        E

that can be lost so easily and simply, like sand slipping through the fingers of Time?

Fake
      Arrogant
           Lost easily and quickly forgotten
                Solid as a straw house
in a whirlwind of emotional turmoil

Reflections on that which did not exist

feelings with True Love **E**asy to confuse sensual, passionate

8 September 2003

Veritable emotional Quest

Take your time
    Righteous
        Understanding and compassionate
            Expect compromises

Laughter
    Open hearts, minds, and whole bodies
        Victory in a cruel and unjust world
            Ecstasy

8 September 2003

Sexual sensationality

Sensual & Spiritual
        Entering new worlds of pleasure
              e**X**citability
                      Undergarments
removed
              A new closeness
      Lotsa music made
Intimacy
      Tantra
           Yin & yang

8 September 2003

Reflective Motherly vibrations

Mother
        Omnicentric
                Theory or Reality?
                        Heart
                Ecosystem
        Rites of Passage

                Elemental & Spiritual Energy
                      Attain tranquility,
peace, & harmony
                Reclaim
        Truth
Hope

9 September 2003

Magnificantlyness of Industrial Hemp

Investigate the history of this magnificent plant
        No deaths after thousands of years of use of its cousin marijuana
            Demand an end to Prohibition that only feeds the prison-military-financial-industrial complex
              Use your mind & see the Truth
            Share your Knowledge with others
        Trade & barter seeds (non-gmo/ge of course)
Respect the Earth from whence we all come from
      Identify the conspirators responsible for the Prohibition (media magnates, industrialists, financiers, government employees – our public servants, and so on)
Organic and BiodynAmic Farming/Gardening for everyone
          Learn the True reasons why this crop has been ill-spoken of

                Heal thyself by what thyself sows
            Educate yourself and others so that this crop can be grown again legally
          Myriad of uses – edible hemp oil & hemp seeds, cloth, cordage, rope, twine, carpet thread, carpet yarn, sailcloth, yarn, cable, string, paper, coarse sheeting, clothing, pressed board, cord, shoes, horse bedding, toweling, artificial sponges, sacking, packing cloth, canvas, necklaces, caulking

Magnificantlyness of Industrial Hemp

People must realize that we do Not need monoculture cash crops, instead we need Biodiversity (wild, cultivated, diverse varieties of "individual crops," mixtures of plants) when we grow this crop – Industrial Hemp – and other plants

Let's move forward and continue GROWING anotha WORLD which is POSSIBLE

For more information, check out:
http://www.questionuniverse.com/oldway/hemp.html
Cannabis sativa L. (Industrial Hemp & Marijuana) Resources

10 September 2003/22 September 2004

11 September: in Retrospection

1 day out of many in which people are murdered by US or our allies
1 day for us to reflect, mourn, bereave, grieve, and realize that we must change

Sow the seeds of forgiveness, truth, peace, and justice
Expect lies from our masters, but demand the Truth
Patriotism or False Pride?
Terrorism – what does it mean? When and how is it used? Illegal wars perhaps?
Explain how anger & hatred solve problems. Isn't that poisoning ourselves?
Maybe change our foreign/domestic perspective & policy -- We have to
Bombings do not solve our problems; only magnify them -- Cycle of Violence.
Everyone is Sacred
Remember 1973 — US-backed/assisted coup of President Salvador Allende in Chile

12 September 2003

Untitled: Us versus Them or People Screwing over Other People (as we all live on one Earth and there is no "us versus them" in the actual Ultimate Reality}

Close your eyes and envision a world full of possibility and freedom

Now reopen your eyes and look at the world around you:
      This ain't it

We've got anotha illegit
President
Time for tha Board of Directors to install a new figurehead
Forget tha voice of da people

They won't react
We gave 'em crack
Can't forget opium and heroin

They know no one's got their back
We gave 'em freedom, they won't move off that couch

They don't realize tha 13th Amendment legalized enslavement for punishment
Can't forget tha Dred Scott case --
Still on tha books

We gave 'em repression and brutality in all forms
They asked for more protection from us by us

Untitled: Us versus Them or People ...

We gave 'em COINTELPRO

They accepted our fairy tale versions of old and new wars at home and abroad
We gave them experiments and forced sterilizations

They don't mind as long as it's Not In Their Backyard – it seems they don't mind if its in their NAME
We allow them to believe they have freedom

They won't fight back if we take it all back
We do it for their sake – in their Name

They want us to spy on their neighbor
We'll deny it if they ask

They will accept our view, they know better
We'll label them "conspiracy theorists" and unpatriotic

They will continue protesting for reforms and not seek real change – Revolution
We'll give them solutions to the symptoms and not the problems

They will ask us to read their e-mails and monitor their conversations – can't be sure who's a "terrorist" and who's not
We will break any and all national and international laws & agreements as we please, in their NAME

They will cheer when we demand their response
We will indefinitely keep their friends, classmates, family

members, neighbors, and fellow global citizens

They will demand their freedoms to be confiscated
We will gladly accept

They will never know the Truth
We'll hide it in "independent" committees that will never get anywhere

They will say 3000 Americans died
We will not challenge that false statement, though we know 3000 or so people died from all over the globe

They will allow and fight in our wars to secure control of tha last drops of oil & gas and clean water
We will wage war to protect them (that's right – them – international financiers and corporate executives)

Did you think we would protect the people?

Remember they gave us back their voice and freedom

We hope they enjoy the economic collapse and the ecological crisis
They won't make us claim responsibility for anything

We will point fingers at tha otha head on this one body politic
They will not accept responsibility – they are only consumers with no freedoms to read, to associate & assemble, to speak freely and to "speak the Truth to Power," and to redress the

Untitled: Us versus Them or People ...

gov'ment in hopes of having a reform in policy

We know it'll take a radical transformation to change the world for tha better. We won't say it for tha public eye though. They will refuse to see this

In the end, those with freedom and those without will realize that we all live on one planet
If we enjoy clean air, water, land, and bodies, then we must reclaim our most basic freedom

The freedom to transform our government and society for tha benefit of all.

We all know ANOTHER WORLD IS POSSIBLE

http://www.senate.gov/civics/constitution_item/constitution.htm
Constitution of the United States

http://www.senate.gov/civics/constitution_item/constitution.htm#amdt_13_(1865)
Amendment XIII (1865)

http://www.archives.gov/exhibits/charters/constitution.html
Constitution of the United States

http://www.archives.gov/exhibits/charters/constitution_amendments_11-27.html
The Constitution: Amendments 11-27

https://en.wikipedia.org/wiki/Thirteenth_Amendment_to_the_United_States_Constitution
Thirteenth Amendment to the United States Constitution
From Wikipedia, the free encyclopedia

https://en.wikipedia.org/wiki/Dred_Scott_v._Sandford
Dred Scott v. Sandford
From Wikipedia, the free encyclopedia

http://rense.com/Datapages/skolnickdatapage.html
America's Great Fairy Tales Part One – 1/10/01 by Sherman H. Skolnick

31 October 2003

Untitled: Did I say sexually frustrated? [Will someone edit this from this book in this society of alleged "freedom"?!)

Sexually frustrated
Spiritually insolvent

She left out as quick as she came
A fantasy, perhaps
Or was it that I could not discern between what was Real and what was not
Did she leave me or did I force her away?
Her fault or mine? Or both of ours?
Who's to say?

I only have memories left to hold on to and she's no longer here to share them with me.
Gone forever out of my Life.

I didn't appreciate her the way that I should have: self-hatred, self-pity, self-doubt, lack of self-control/discipline
I didn't see the signs that she was slipping out of my fingers
I figured that I could always have her, she wouldn't have the strength to leave.
Shit, I was wrong or what?
Didn't expect that to happen.

Wishing my days could be brighter
Wishing for the memories to come alive again
Wishing for the strength to move on and move forward

Untitled: Did I say sexually frustrated?

Wishing for the wisdom to forgive her and myself
Wishing for the answers to the questions: Why?
        What could I have done better?
        What can I do now?
        What should I do now?

So I continue to sit here sexually frustrated
No longer able to inundate my partner with my steamy, liquid blessings
No longer able to feel that connection – like I've lost a part of myself
No longer able to experience her sexual prowess

I sit here wanting to blame someone else for my temporary disconnection
Yet I can't, I did it all myself to myself
I was with anotha good person and once again I fucked up – my ego and I destroyed our happiness

So I sit here wandering why I am sittin' here sexually frustrated when there is a Life to live and people to meet

I guess the pain of recognizing my own culpability is too great
Or maybe it's that I hope that she'll come back
Or that she'll accept me back
Or maybe I'm still too stunned to see Reality through my eyes clouded with tears

Sexually frustrated, missing the mental stimulation as much as the vaginal penetration

Untitled: Did I say sexually frustrated?

And the full bodily excitation and relaxation

Exotic massages
Fulfilling fantasies
Love – so painful when it's so False – full of lies and deceit
Though I know it was False Love, the pain still exists

Attempt suicide to relieve the pain and heart-ache
May solve that problem, but won't be able to see anotha day of sunshine and realize that I'm blessed
Plus it would create other problems
Do I love myself that little to die over False Love?
Is she worth dying for?
Am I worth living for?
Am I afraid of living or am I afraid of dying?

I can't think that deeply profound now,
Remember I'm sexually frustrated

I miss the closeness
Sex is more than a physical art, much more
The more you know about sex, the more you know about your partner & yourself

I hope that you don't fall victim to False Love
I hope that I don't fall victim again to False Love
I am a Survivor sitting here for now, sexually frustrated, until I take responsibility for myself and realize that this cycle will continue until I break it.
Or I can always sit here by myself and think of the memories and

ask myself why I'm sexually frustrated.

31 October 2003

Untitled: Alone and Angry?

ALONE

or just lonely

How can one feel lonely or be alone in a crowd?☹
How and why have we accepted this most devastating cost, just so that we can live in a ~~free~~ slave, capitalistic country?
How can we see each other not ~~as people~~ as competitors (for consumption/over consumption, approval, victimhood status as the most oppressed group, academic grades, and so on), but as brothers and sisters within the universal Web of Life?
How can we change this false sense of Reality?
How can we reConnect to the environment within us and around us?
How can we say that we are the most intelligent beings if we limit our ideas to three (3) systems of economics & societal governance? Does this confining further compound our loneliness?

One system out of many
I sit here utterly   ALONE

Untitled: Alone and Angry?

I don't get it though
I live in a large residence and
still these emotions persist
In this place where I reside
there are spirits, other animals (insects, rodents, and so on), and
of course various noxious
toxic chemicals
Outside one can hear the "triumphant"
sounds of progress (destruction at any cost)
in the automobiles and trucks
and sometimes sounds of ongoing progress:
CONSTRUCTION (control, manipulation, and destruction at any cost)
So how can I feel lonely in this
PRISON?
either of my own doing or that was afforded to me
Though I hear the sounds of the birds singing as a new day in this
particular time, place, and space emerges to the forefront
and when the day comes to an end there is the
serenading of the musical bats devouring fruits and insects of all kinds
and the ballads of the crickets just around me
How can I be   ALONE
here?
Is it just me?
Am I too much of an individual?
Is it because I can not see the larger perspective, thanks to the
multitude of lights that block out the stars which lit the path to a
presumed freedom (even if only temporary) for my ancestors
(who called upon me to continue on the struggle for equality &

Untitled: Alone and Angry?

justice)?
Is it because I can no longer track the movements of these lovely celestial beings (the sun, moon, stars, other planets, and UFOs) so that I can better understand my place in this world and how I am truly affected by their presence (or lack thereof)?
Is it due to not being able to have the winds flowing thru my closed window and closed-off body (except for my wild, engaging hair, of course)?
Is it because I have self-imposed a stunting of my own personal beliefs, visions, dreams, Realities, nightmares, quests, emotions, and Connections to the greater Universes around me so that I could seem partially "normal?"
What in the world does that mean anyways – "normal?"
    Who determines that and why?
    What is "normal" to one is not necessarily "normal" to ALL.
Do my feelings come from the lack of clean wind, Earth, bodies, water, and so on?
    Isn't that a freedom we ALL should cherish?

Trying to block out the immense beauty of the sky by making higher and higher structural contraptions will only make us more lonely.
Vilifying those that would hug trees or other non-human beings will only make us more lonely.
We should embrace the wisdom of the ancient ones (rocks and bacteria) and learn from them that we can not be alone in such a place.

Our Creators are within and around us always.

Untitled: Alone and Angry?

How can one of immense material affluence be so lonely and in despair to choose the option of suicide?
How can we instill in our children and their children and their children and their children and their children and their children and their children the belief that we are
not   ALONE
and should not be lonely in such a place, time and space?
There are worlds all around us and within us.
I can not be alone, for I am not an individual, but one of many. It is WE and not I. Thank-you: To all my guides in the various dimensions, realms, and worlds of the Universes.

We ALL must understand what our unique purpose and contribution is to the evolution of Life on this planet, our Mother the Earth.

We are alone no more.
We are lonely no more.

How can one feel like one belongs, yet one is still empty inside?
What can fill in this emptiness – this spiritual void?
Are you spiritually starved too?

What can we DO?
Even when we feel lonely or are alone, we never truly are. It just seems that way.
Ya know, Life is just funny that way sometimes.

Untitled: Alone and Angry?

We don't understand what's
going on
Until much later in our
journeys.
We guess it's just the way
the Universe revolves and evolves.

##

Depression and thoughts of suicidal
attractions creep into the hidden
chambers of my mental ware
like shadows free to reappear in the world
after their time of rest in their
hidden abodes.
These feelings do not wish to be shaken
or thrown out
they seem to have attached themselves
to the very walls of my mental chambers
and thus are ingrained in my daily
ritual of sleep & face a bleak Reality
where I walk around   aLone
Yes I do feel connected to the non-human beings around me
though I must be crazy, insane, or mentally
deranged to feel such emotions, thoughts, and feelings
according to some of our most prestiged and esteemed human
beings

Do I feel connected to other human beings?
I do NOT know.

Untitled: Alone and Angry?

What do U feel?
Do U feel that I do or could belong?
Will I have to change who I am to belong to this exclusive club?

Pain emerges as the main mental picture
as I continue on my Trek around empty
vessels who seem to not know the
current Reality that they must be
immune or unaware of.
I think to myself, these are the future presidents, lawyers,
business owners, and machines/cogs in the exploitative system
that we've helped create, enforce, and/or support over the years.

Having mounds of thoughts to leak out to
hopefully engage and ¡WAKE Up! ☺ the empty
vessels not Realizing *The Matrix* is all
around us.
Not simply a movie, but an accurate depiction of what exists and
will exist for us
UNLESS
we determine a better future for ourselves that empowers and
engages
each of us in developing our fullest potential

Hope can not be lost though, as those that I may feel are Asleep
may actually be more in-tune and AWAKE
than I assume and believe
that I AM. ☺
Who knows?

Untitled: Alone and Angry?

The loneliness felt by one
who's designed his/her own
PRISON
and is filled with negative karmic energy from many years of flourishing
without a soul (walking around ALIVE, yet dead spiritually and emotionally with no conscience)
may not be understood by others who
have never had to experience such
a tragic tale of drama and trauma
as this being regains his/her soul and
faces the nightmarish visions of
knowing what one has done to others
and realizing that the position that he/she
currently occupies is his/her own fault and not that of others.
It must be difficult for that one to accept such responsibility
and this story is not likely to be repeated
as others may not believe that
"a cup filled with tea that breaks does not diminish the fact that the tea still exists, though in anotha form" (the Essence of Reincarnation).
What drives us to want to feel Connected to others and want to belong to the greater family that extends beyond the human family?
What drives one to wish to live the Life
of a hermit, separate from the presence
of other human beings?

The prison that he/she created was

Untitled: Alone and Angry?

designed and built for a reason or for
various reasons.
Will others who see this being wonder and seek to understand
his/her predicament?
Limiting oneself to others that share a similar consciousness
brings forth loneliness and feelings of despair when those
selected to be in this circle do not continue to fit within the
confines prescribed for membership in the close-knit group?
Will opening oneself up to others bring forth
laughs of ridicule or grated teeth with
negative flashes of energy of scorn and
contempt for what is slowly, yet deliberately
driven out from one's mental chambers
to the air waves of sound outside one's
corporeal body so that another
being can hear this story, which one
has hidden so skillfully for so long?
What does all this mean?

Is the author suffering from another mental hallucination again?
Does the writer need psychological assistance for the psychosis
present here?

The prisoner who architects her/his own bed must therefore
sleep in it.
Right?
Or should the prisoner share her/his own burdens with others
that may or may not exist around her/him?

In a societal of artificial personalities and

responses, can it be believed that one will
meet someone that is completely and
accurately Real? ☺ ☹
Or are we ALL so impressed upon by
the society that we must change that we,
from time to time, act as if we never
doubted the scenario of falsity that society
drafted for us and instilled in us:
through our parents, peers, schools, the media, government, and so on?
Maybe all of this is irrelevant since we all believe that material wealth will solve ALL of the
Problems in the world today:

Hopefully the esoteric, ethereal, exotic thoughtful contemplations presented throughout will not diminish Ur belief of the superiority of this consumerist, machine-like, robotic, exploitative, genocidal/murderous, arrogant, spiritually empty society.
That is for those of us that reside within the confines of the Constitutional Republic of the United States of America.

The being possessed with thoughts, ideas, emotions, feelings, dreams, nightmares, visions, hallucinations, and such not prescribed by society as being "normal" fits into what group within the greater society?
As aforementioned, there is not separation, so just because one's level of consciousness is on a higher or lower level does not keep one from being a part of the Universal cosmological family that binds us ALL.

Untitled: Alone and Angry?

If one was to look only at the differences
and forget that we are All the same
at the most fundamental and basic level
of existence, then that one would be
only one.
However, when that being recognizes that
we ALL are energy and recognizes that we
exist within a truly, interconnected Web of
Life, then that one being sees that she/he is
not ₐₗₒₙₑ, for there is no individual,
only ALL of us.
Yet this does not destroy nor limit our individuality and
uniqueness.
Just 'cause we are all fundamentally the
same, does not mean that there are not
differences.
The objective is to recognize both the similarities and differences
exist within a harmonious balance.

The one that built her/his prison can revoke
what he/she engineered and open up her/his
heart to have compassion and reinvigorate the
ReConnection to all beings within the
Universal Order.

But, what if one does not wish to accept that he/she does not
have to live within a prison built by his/her own hands?
That is a good question that we ALL may need to
discuss.
What do U Think?

Untitled: Alone and Angry?

###

I feel for tha old being trapped within
the body of a young being.
Actually that should be tha old soul (Spirit).
The young body/old soul connection does not
exist for most of us in terms of our plausible
mental Realities of actual physical, interpretative
possibilities.
Whatever all that means? ☺ ☹

The duo feels left out of young circles and old circles at the same
time, traversing between the two camps as if a buoy floating
around in the ocean riding the waves being pushed in different
directions by the gentle and turbulent waves of water particles.
How it must feel to realize that one does
not fit in the world, yet still feels intimately
connected to the same world that one does not
belong in.
It must be similar to the person
who leaves home for a journey and
returns home realizing that she/he is
no longer the same as when she/he left.
Thus, feeling misplaced as those she/he
encounters have not experienced what he/she
has and thus cannot accurately surmise the
reasons for his/her change: transformation and growth.

Oh how it must feel to live in the same

Untitled: Alone and Angry?

world as others, yet still not live in the
same world as others.

I feel the pain and anguish of the one who
feels that he/she cannot be properly understood
as others can not fathom the experiences that
this particular being has experienced.
The visions of Reptilians trekking around the physical
realm of this world do not occur to most, but
or this being – these are the many faces of
Reality.
Should this being slither back into the Nether World or into the
Dream World to exist within his/her proper time, space, and
place?
It could be that those that don't understand
have mounds of Cosmic Dust on their psyches
and thus can not accurately view the world
from their Third Eyes.

It could be that the being described above and
the writer of this work are just suffering from
mental delusions and are really just crazy and
have been inducing stress-related mental hallucinations
to add personality to the areas of Life where
that aspect is lacking.

I hope that he/she understands that we are
only interpreters of the world that we see
and experience and thus we view others
through our own eyes and not through their

Untitled: Alone and Angry?

eyes.

Imagine seeing someone how they see themselves
and imagine seeing yourself through someone else's
eyes.

Is one who can not or will not open
up his/her-self to others and thus occupies
outside of the realm of most human
actions alone or just lonely?

Can the lonely or alone being open up his/her consciousness so
as to allow/accept others into his/her circular embrace?

Oh how it feels to have a warm embrace from someone that you
care about deeply and/or that cares about you deeply.
However, for some of us that is just a dream that will never fully
actualize itself in a physical Real world, but may occur within the
Dream World.
How does giving a warm embrace feel to you? ☺
Giving of myself more than what I receive
has depleted my reserves of energy that never
really existed anyway – just as I don't
really exist either.
I'm only someone's figment, fragmented imaginative
responsive to a dilemma that did not exist,
yet the imaginer believes occurred.

Embracing the embrace of oneself attempting
to clarify deeply-held thoughts, without

Untitled: Alone and Angry?

sacrificing one's own consciousness to ridicule
and scorn as one can not take the criticism
whence so little supportive positive flows of
energy are not present to counterbalance
the effective negativity.

The old spirit in the young body cries out,
yet no one hears the tears nor sees the
gritty stains of dried saline excretions from the
ocular, optical illusionary instrumentations.

I guess this poet/writer has issues of
intellectualizing everything that comes around
his/her way.
What kind of poem is this?☹

Maybe he/she should check him/her-self into a
mental hospital and waste away there.
However don't worry, they'll kick him/her out
due to his/her lack of insurance.
Thus he/she will have the opportunity
to join the millions of people living on the
streets in the cities of the
world.
No one would miss him/her as he/she
did not exist to the world anyway.
The wonder could not fathom a comprehen-
sion of this enigmatic, socially passive and
socially left out sinister person with great hope
and great despair.

Untitled: Alone and Angry?

But, who cares?☹☺☹

I'll return this instrument of scribing back
to the hands of the poet/writer
deciphering this influx of mental, psychic
musical notes into some sort of
plausible description of collected words
found in a single syntax.

Viewing a sky filled with the vibrant
colors of a sunset, signaling the coming
of the night sky and the easy ability
to view the moon, planets, and stars
fills this one up with happiness as this
one sees what Life is about: a circular,
cyclic system of balancing Life and Death. ☺

####

Only an idiot tries to love one more than he/she
Tries to love him/herSelf
Only an idiot mistakes lust or False Love for True Love
And continues to seek the falsity though one knows it will only
lead to unhappiness, feelings of hatred towards that "person"
though the fault lies squarely with him/herSelf
Is it possible that the idiot doesn't Realize that she/he is an idiot chasin' an ideal or dream
that can never be reached, as tha dream
was False to begin with.

Untitled: Alone and Angry?

You're probably thinking to Urself right now:
Is the being responsible for these words feeling like an idiot?
Thus, are these personal, rather than impersonal feelings?
Would it be bad for me to laugh at this
IDIOT? ☺
How can one with soooo much knowledge and intelligence fail so miserably at love and relationships?
What's wrong with this being?

What one interprets these words as, one
does
This particular being does not wish to force an interpretation on
U
though this particular being has done a fair
share of such actions over time.
Oh well.
Contradictory insultations relationally, mystically,
non-rationality contextualizations of a matter
representing wave-particles energy dynamical
proportionalities.

In the distance, a being sits alone with
no visible human beings in sight
U think to Urself: What is wrong with her/him?
What would drive someone to divest him/herSelf from the human-centered world?
        Relationships with significant others, friends or families
        Farcical, superficial social "Reality" (Fakeland)

Untitled: Alone and Angry?

                Political Malcontent
                Reconnecting with the Universes around and
within us
                Escaping criminal prosecution and attempting to
fully listen to one's conscience to offer a plausible solution based
on restoration
                Trying to step away from other human beings so
full of drama and trauma
                Living with the seasonal vibrations and temporal
fluctuations
One may think to his/herSelf that I/we
could be there just as well as that particular
being
as tha troubles of modern-living are just getting
too much to take seriously and not be under
the influence of appeasing biochemical addictions to shut
down and shut out the idiocy around OneSelf
Maybe these words are only just jumping off
the page and into your mental chambers and
these ideas are not floating through your head
investing themselves as your thoughts
as if any One of us has our own, unique thoughts that are utterly
new and original.
What we do, say, and/or think has most likely
been done, said, and/or thought before by someone
else so we are not as special as we may
try to make ourselves out to be afterall.

Do not let me take your shine.
Do not let me take your pleasure.

Untitled: Alone and Angry?

Do not let me take your love.
Do not let us take Ur soul.
Do not let us destroy our Universe.

Remember however bad you may think U have it
that there is someone who may have it even
worse
Be blessed for what U have
and do not
have

I don't have her
I can't have her
I want to have her
I can't possess her
I don't even possess myself
I know my very premise of trying to possess her or myself is a
root of my own suffering, pain, and agony
Simply self-afflicted relational wounds that
will go away with time if only
I remember the lessons from each
relationship as I enter into the next
Well remember and practice what I know

Why are relationship so hard?
Why do I want to be with other human beings, yet want to be
separated from them?
Why do we feel these emotions?
Why do we want to be alone when we cry and are depressed
and yet wish to be in the company

Untitled: Alone and Angry?

of others when we are happy and joyful?
Why do we give so much of ourselves to others when we receive
so little in return?
Breaking our own hearts so that we can
be lonely and wallow in our own agony over
being alone.
The person sitting alone probably does not understand
this presence and thus decided to withdraw --
whether temporarily or permanently so as not
to hopefully fall under the spell of this
idiocy

Love when Love
Truly exists
can be the most Beautiful
of all the emotions, dreams, and ideas
that we possess,
yet do not possess
Tears of joy wallow down the soft-spoken
epidermal layer of skin causing a reaction of
more saline excretions as tha burnin'
sensation continues and U wonder if all of
this is really Real or if it was just a
dream that was embraced upon and not ever
actualized
so it only remains an empty promise of something that does not
exist
not even within Ur mind
Yet it still happened
As you remember what it feels to be filled with Love

Untitled: Alone and Angry?

and be in the presence of others, no longer
aLone and lonely. ☺
Oh what a joy that must truly be.
When you have that, don't be such an idiot
to believe he/she will always be around when
you treat them like shit
Treat them well
They should treat you well

Loneliness is only a temporary abstraction of
a depressional ideology rooted within itself,
yet prominent within the physical manifestations
that we involve ourselves within
Lose the loneliness and fill up Ur heart
with positivity and all that is negative
will go away

We each determine whether we will be happy or sad
We each determine whether we will be alone and/or lonely
           We each determine how we will deal with such
occurrences in our lives
The being sitting alone looks at the
reflection in the glowingly, radiant river
with the magnamous sun shining brightly behind
him/her and in the reflection, I see the being
and it is ME. We are One and the SAME.

#####

Jammin' to an archetypal sound of

Untitled: Alone and Angry?

lonely voices murmurin' in my mental dome
A$_L$ONE and lonely at the same time trapped in a cellular, molecular, subatomic, superstringest complex of interactions within a body politic that can be seen by those "on the outside trying to peer in" to which they choose not or just can not comprehend as it jumbles up their static worldview of how the Universes are supposed to operate on scientific-rationalism based laws and assumptions of mechanical thinking or on an "us' versus "them" religiosity that limits the Universal view in a static, mechanical mannerism.

Therefore, how can what I presuppose as the condition or order of beings to which I belong exist if the 2 major facets of worldly knowledge precludes that my thoughts are either irrational or blasphemous.

What one views as Reality is mostly controlled and manipulated by one's own Perception. But, from where does Perception come from?
Where does consciousness come from?
Where does the fundamental struggle of good versus evil ("us" versus "them") arrive from?

If what we now believe to be a modern, medical science were to undergo a drastic transformation to a more modern, yet ancient archetypal view, as occurred in chemistry & physics some 80 – 100 years ago in a Gregorian calendar system, then would that

Untitled: Alone and Angry?

also help us re-Perceive ourselves and our relationship to each other? Just some random, passing thoughts so don't pay attention to these misguided thoughts.

Does anyone know how lonely it is to exist in a world that does not allow for one's full existence in a state so accustomed to shouting about how much supposed "freedom" that exists?
Anger or pain, blood or tears stain
the conscience of one born yet with one
and without one.
Abstract or concrete or at a state
that does not differentiate between these
presumed extremes.
We are more similar than we are
different, yet we allow ourselves to be
DIVIDED and
CONQUERED.

######

ANGRY?☹
¡¿Am I angry?☹ ☺

Am I disturbed that the heartbeat of our Mother -- the Earth -- has been quelched and quieted?
        What heartbeat?
Tha Drums of Africa, Asia, Australia, Europe, and the Americas.
        Da rhythms and beats linking our sisters, aunts, mothers, and so on to the Original Woman/Womyn and our terrestrial/celestial Mother (Mama, Madre}.

Untitled: Alone and Angry?

Tha rhythm was crushed because we were "pagan," strange religious believers and da drums empowered womyn too. [Can't do that -- Can we??}

Tears stumble down my cheek, they belong to the Earth. As we all do.

Anger – a venomous poison that toxifies the Body of his/her assumed possessor.
Must find a way to turn this poison into positive, creative energies to fully acquaint mySelf with tha love our Mother/Father hath bestowed to us.

But, how can I be full of anger at what *they* hath done to da Earth and ultimately to ourSelves?

How can I be angry, if I speak of peace
and purpose and love?

How can I be a potential Revolutionary force
OR outlet (depending on Ur perspective] and
still have human frailties and weaknesses?

How can I speak of eye?

¡Is not there only WE?

Ancient peoples and current peoples have determined that bodies can exist in two, 3, four, or more states of being/existence at da same time.

How?

Light exists as both a particle and a wave. Beyond that, every molecule of the Universes has consciousness as we all exist as fundamental energies of differing levels and intensities.

Remember that there exist several parallel and at times opposing Realities, Universes, dimensions, realms, worlds, and so on.

Remember that we are fundamentally more similar than we are different.

A belief in inclusivity.
We are ultimately interconnected and interrelated
          Through superstrings.

This being speaking to U through this being writing encoded cryptics is not nor wishes to be Perfect.
We are good <u>and</u> bad.
        Do not expect us to be Perfect.
        Expect us to make mistakes and to
                continuously improve.

The connective tissues of the "Web of Life"

Untitled: Alone and Angry?

keep us stranded in the same Reality, though we may try and escape to a Real Existence through drugs or other intoxicants in this age of FalseNess and OverConsumption patterns that may spell our very own demise at our very own Hands.

We can only blame ourselves.
        We can only change ourselves.
        We must save ourselves to save our terrestrial Mother/Father.

We must imagine the possibilities.

We must break out of our alienation & loneliness in this capitalistic society.

We all must think of alternatives:

        Sustainable, local economies
            Agriculture [biodynamic & organic]
                Communities
                Governance
        Society
        Trading & bartering
        Permaculture
        Research TRUE sustainability, not tha co-opted versions

Believe in the possibilities and empower UrSelf to Dream
Allow Urself to remove Urself from "the box"

Untitled: Alone and Angry?

Ask: Do we *really* Need <u>More</u>?

Unleash your own creative juices.

#######

Is what I hath scribed
        -- Poetry? ☺ ☹
For it does not rhyme
It is not epic in proportions
It is not simply continuous
There are just 2 many questions
Is it even creative?

¿How do you (re)define poetic aspirational aspectals?
What criterion emulates Ur perspective glance?

Poetry is a voice, we all have this voice, yet
we all display that in numerous ways.
Even my/our own voice is not simply the same
at all times within this particular stated single
poetry example.

Who can (or should] judge the work(s} of another
fellow being?
Does it hath not take bravery to present oneself
to the Universes as a Creative Soul?

We have hoped to inspire dialogue, action, and consciousness-
raising from the blended rhythmic notations ascribed to these

Untitled: Alone and Angry?

particular pages.

In this way, hopefully we {as da authors] will also embody this change that is sought within this Earthly realm.
Thus, we hope that we try more so to constantly improve continually & practice what positive vibes that we send out there.

Yet, what is this "there" that is referenced?
¿¡Is not this just too abstractional and enigmatic.?!
Could this be anotha case of [over)intellectualizing of the predicament within the globe through using "big words" and hard-to-define and understand concepts and philosophies.

Please do Not forget hard-to-follow patterns of thought.
That would be a shame if it was forgotten.

To forget to love oneself is not an expression that one wishes to deal with within a context that tries not to limit nor simplify complex interactions between all systems within and around the system known as tha human body.

Is not it amazing how sexual beings become not only asexual, but functionally unable to C that sexuality is a part of our very being & Essence

Untitled: Alone and Angry?

(Spirituality)? Maybe, it's just us again.

Sexuality is only one of our links to the Creative Forces/Beings that brought us into existence.
Yes, sex and sexuality is a <u>creative</u> endeavor.

Sex - the taboo that continues to harken us to reconfigure how we fit ourselves into the puzzle of the mysterious Universes.

Sexual, emotional, physical, mental/intellectual, occupational, Spiritual, psychic, and so on are just some of the spheres of Health/Wellness/Well-Being that we must entertain within the matrix of the Health of the Universes, Milky Way Galaxy, stars, planets, Moon, Sun, Earth, our nation, local biological region (bioregion}, family, community, and thus ourSelves.

Our Health is thus dependent on the Creative Balancing Acts (Universal Dances) of the known/unknown dimensions of existEnce.

The ancient wisdoms will complement the so-called newfound knowledge and this convergence will allow us to see alternative paths to keep us from impending Doom & Destruction due to our own ignorance due to our arrogance and our individualistic, human-centered selfishness which we have used to cut ourSelves off from the understanding of how the Sexual Creativity of the Universe is not relegated to only human beings,

however it is a quintessential aspect of the
Life-bearing "Web of Life."

The human odyssey must be to figure our
place in the Universe in our particular
time, space, and place (place-based consciousness).

What is the Ultimate purpose of our
breathing?
How we will be(come] Significant and not simply
a success?

Digestible nutritional intellectual grams of
odorable plasmic perfunctory patterns of linguistic
relationships encoded within a precept notion of
arrangeable symbols and notations delivered to your
mental dome in just one of tha Imperial
Languages (in this particular case -- English).

Continuously fragmenting the effable langual component
to expand a dire need to reinvigorate a discussion
of enhancing the words currently tritely used, yet
lacking multiple syntactical meanings at different
levels of consciousness

We hope that U've enjoyed the words scribbled
and tha illustrative momentos displayed to enhance
tha effect and da experience. ☺

########

Untitled: Alone and Angry?

Life is abundant, even within the area
of the Earth between my outstretched legs
Maple seedlings - the helicopters of our Youth and childhood
so full of vigor, innocence, and potential
(Am I referring to the Maple seedlings or our Youth? Or could the
referring amusal be towards both?)
Tree limbs (sticks)
clovers
ants (what species?) foraging
moss
Which direction -- sacred direction am I facing?
Which sacred direction is facing towards me?
North?
South?
East?
West?

Feel the wind blow currents of fluids through the tangled, yet
untangled portions of my braided (controlled) mane
Listening to the sounds of pollution coming from anthropogenic
sources and functions
Listening to the birds communicating to
each other in a language that I have
yet to decipher
watching a couple of brown squirrels
(another of our descriptions - not their own)
playfully jest in a relatively open green
and brown area

Untitled: Alone and Angry?

Left the prison-fortress (school) to breathe
a sigh of relief in an unenclosed
habitable region of time and space
Looking for answers, yet asking more
questions

When was the last time cold morning
dew softened the monstrous print of the
foot's path on a hurried journey to a
known and expected destination

Whatever happened to the diligent
patience allowing for slow movements and
for reflection apon Creation around us,
within us, and occurring all within their
own time

Reminiscent tales of laughter and tears
of sadness and joy stain the facial tissues
as the long day full of vibrant sun's lit
dreams age on

Wishing that the subtlety of living to Live
for joy and purpose would simply replace
or even erase Living for Jobs/school
one's purpose is surely much more than the
latter,
Right?

Though one can not see with our naked,

Untitled: Alone and Angry?

unaided eyes, worms, microorganisms, and a plethora
of teeming beings live beneath my body sitting
upon the Earth, watching the shadows
grow longer and stiller as day here turns to night fall
providing a better glimpse of the Moon
than during the day perhaps

This may be the best expressions of freedom,
being in the midst of an evolving Creation and
having no control to make these events into
my own vision

Let be what will be

Radical roots pull me back closer to my
Earthly, spiritual mother as she shows me
the paths which lay upon her body
Realizing that with so many choices, many
thoughts must be filtered through
or simply I could just Live and not
force what is not meant to be
Just let be what shall be

Allow for the Earth to heal Herself and
ye too shall heal too
Allow for Her to grow as wild and
full as possible and ye all shall be rewarded finely

White
Violet

Untitled: Alone and Angry?

Shades of green
Shades of brown
Shades of yellow
Shades of black

For these are the colors of my constant
memories of walking barefoot and barelegged
around la tierra - mi madre (the Earth - my
Mother in Spanish)

Robust litanies of flying insects dispersed
by flailing objects from threes – seedlings or
leaves, perhaps, falling down at an
acceleration subjective to Newton's
gravitational pull, perhaps (maybe) one day we'll
know how accurate such a muddled
approximation could be

Love is in the air, this Love can be
smelled and felt by all as the gentleness
or turbulence of the winds pass all around
us in a myriad of directions

Trying to make a poem like yours, like
the last one, can't happen like that all tha
time.

Sitting here reliving the anger pageant of
my dreams
We sit on the sidelines as tha triumphant

musical interludes of the marching bands
announces the coming of the paraders apon
the starkly heat-receiving engineering pavement of sorts
There was anger with passion wearing some
ridiculously ravageous revolting ridiculed red-like restive vest
There was anger with flowers- a dozen
red and white wilted roses screaming out for
some affection, some attention
ANYTHING
There was anger with no heading back -
harsh words were appallingly courted in multiple
directions with neither being wishing to
take responsibility for the havoc that
each one has now been put through

There was anger with green envy and
jealously -- speaking on the conditions of
anonymity about how better dressed and all
that that this particular parader was than all tha
others assembled in this momentous
celebratory cause of negative emotional
feedback

Reflecting back on the journey to the
"Great Outdoors"
places me in a different tonal mood, filled
up with hope and passion, not resentful,
suppressed relics of anger unresolved

Did you listen to the winds?

Untitled: Alone and Angry?

What did you hear?
Did you listen to the trees?
What knowledge did they bring you?
Did you listen to the birds?
What songs did they sing to you?
Did you listen to the Universe(s)?
What messages did they bring you?
Did you listen to the ancestors?
What hope did they send you?
Did you really listen?

Close your eyes and open up your full
heart and listen again
Not for me
Do it 4 UrSelf
Do it 4 tha Future
Look beyond UrSelf
Open up UrSelf
Love ThySelf
Quiet the chatter of your mind, close
the racing tracks and be still and
quiet so that U can hear what
they're trying to say to U.

Be appreciative for what U have been
bestowed and blessed to be stewards of, please
do not take this to mean: Destroy, dominate,
and control.
Let it mean be cognizant of the complexity, respect true
biodiversity, respect and honor all Life, allow for balance, and

Untitled: Alone and Angry?

recognize evolutionary adaptability in all of Creation.

The winds are blowing good tidings and blessings
in this here direction as this one poem comes
to a close while striving for the rootedness of an
ancient Sequoia so high up in the sky and deeply rooted
in our common Mother. Listen to my woes of loneliness
and see that will Life all around, NO one is truly lonely or alone.

\# 19 November 2003
\#\# 7 December 2003 Deux Parte
\#\#\# 8 December 2003 Tripartical
\#\#\#\# 10 December 2003 4
\#\#\#\#\# 21 January 2004 Pentaful
\#\#\#\#\#\# 7 February 2004 Sat-ur-Day
\#\#\#\#\#\#\# 15 February 2004 Untitled
\#\#\#\#\#\#\#\# 18 April 2004 Radicaleth

Life in the Barrel

We live in a barrel, a large, living, and breathing barrel teaming with biological and cultural diversity, to be more exact. There is nothing wrong with that.

In this barrel, there appeared a species of Life some time ago. This species of life has existed for approximately 0.087% (eighty-seven thousandths of a percent) [1] of the total time that the barrel has existed. The barrel has continuously provided sustenance for those living within Her/Him and ultimately created from Him/Her, including the particular beings that are being referred to. Anyways, this species emigrated around the barrel to various places over many, many, many, many years.

Over time, some members of this species of Life created a brave, new ideology that viewed the barrel that supported them and all other beings within the barrel as synonymous to mechanical clocks created by that species of Life and thus could be broken apart and analyzed as separate entities. Thus, the barrel and all Life within this barrel were no longer revered and thus "anything goes." Also, because of the separation, there was no longer wholeness and thus a sense of responsibility for the well-being of all as you are interconnected and interrelated to all.

Those who created this ideology were not content to just destroy the area of the barrel where they lived, provided that those who ruled (or at least believed themselves to be in that position of power and dominance) could afford the luxury of sending out from their bosom interested parties of "scientific and cultural expeditionists" (marauders, invaders, missionaries, civilizers, treasure seekers, enslavers, etc.) who would gather information about the world around them for their particular King or Queen that would be useful in successfully classifying others of this particular species (imperialistic capitalist expansions to gather needed "natural resources" and enslaved peoples to feed the means to spread this new found message around the barrel). (This is not to say that others within this species were not already operating out of this or a similar mind frame. Please continue on with the story to find out more.)

How did this small fractional percentage of the whole entire species determine or come to an understanding that all members of this species had to become believers in the ideology put forth by them? (The rulers felt that they were not affected by the catastrophic and destructive changes that they made to their particular area, they were, even if they weren't going to admit it. Everyone in that area was acquiescent and complicit in the destruction of their particular area through ignorance, denial, active participation, and/or other means/methods.)

Over the course of time, $1.09e^{-05}$% of the total time that the barrel has been alive [2], some members of this species of Life, which destroyed their own area of the barrel, have touched virtually every area of the barrel and has forced this ideology through various means (coercion/extortion, assimilation, acculturation, through religious disguise, and so on) on others in this particular species of Life. Thus, in an inconsequential amount of time, relative to the full time of the barrel's existence and growth/development, this whole particular species has enabled themselves to make Life unbearable not only for themselves through violent acts (pollution, poverty, rape, War--

terrorism, hatred, manipulation/control, greed, etc.), but they have also managed to come to a tumultuous moment in the history not only of their own species, but also of the barrel and Her/His other inhabitants.

It has been determined by some of this species of Life that all beings that have existed within this barrel can be lost forever, within the next $1.09e^{-06}$% to $2.17e^{-06}$% of the total time [3] that the barrel has been providing Herself/Himself to ALL inhabitants, not just that particular species of Life. Isn't it great that we don't live within that barrel and we aren't a part of that species of Life?

Who is responsible for the possible, eventual fate of the totality of Life in that barrel? (That is if they refuse to transform themselves by first changing their perception.) Who in that particular species of Life is responsible for the possible, eventual fate of the barrel and Her/His inhabitants -- some of the species of Life that started this ideology and passed it along over generations around to the other members of the species living in other areas of the barrel? Are the other members of this species of Life that acquiesced in this nightmare [through denial; ignorance; inactive and/or active participation; willful, active and/or inactive participation] and did not speak up nor out and did not engage in consciously thinking and behaving contrary to the dominating belief of that species of Life complicit in their shared Fate and thus partially responsible as well?

This same story can be told in a more concise manner.

We live in a barrel, sort of like apples in a barrel. If there is a problem with any of the apples in the barrel, just simply remove them (assassinations, Wars -- terrorism, send them to prisons and concentration camps, etc.) and the problem goes away. Right? Once the "bad" apple(s) is/are removed, then peace, justice, love & harmony will return to the barrel and all the apples will remain in that perpetual state since the "bad" apples were removed. WRONG!

The problem lays in the fact that this barrel is falling apart at the seams. The sides and bottom are falling apart. Even so, the constant cry and demand are for the "bad" apples to be removed so that they don't affect the other apples in this barrel. As the inside of the barrel gets hotter and hotter over time, the barrel continues to fall apart and the apples themselves are beginning to fall out of place, thus out of the barrel. The apple picker doesn't notice this fact and continues taking the "bad" apples out of the barrel to avoid contamination of the other "good" apples.

One day the barrel breaks and all the apples fall out and thus the apple picker now has to get rid of all of the apples and the barrel. This barrel needed to be fixed (brought back in balance) a long time before the barrel eventually collapsed and broke completely apart.

In the world today, we keep saying that we should just take the "bad" apples out of the political process and then the other apples will be fine as we continue on our merrily way avoiding responsibility at all levels and at any cost. As well, we fail to realize that the problems that we think that we are solving today are only the symptoms of a problem that has its roots in our shared consciousness. (It is important to note here that not everyone shares this consciousness, which is great!!)

The barrel is the Earth/Sky/Heavens (Universal Cosmos) and we are/can be the apples and/or the apple picker. We choose which role we play at different times in different places. Sometimes we make the easy choice to be ignorant and other times we make the more difficult choice of being actively engaged and trying to get to the root of our problems. Instead of focusing solely on the apples that are considered to be "bad," we also need to focus on the collective Fate of the apples that are in a barrel that will no longer continue to sustain the apples. We are in the midst of great turmoil and an overwhelming ecological crisis, which in turn is interconnected and interrelated to our overall societal world crisis.

Each of us has played a part in these crises by our own passive, active, indirect, and/or direct participation. As well, some have refused to play a part in the global charade, the false notion that limitless expansion and exploitation of the Earth and all of her inhabitants could progress uninterrupted forever without any negative consequences to those who believe that they are the winners in the game of Life. At the same time, many others wanted to enter this brand of the game of Life, not realizing that they too by their own acquiescence as tools (consumers, labor, etc.) were partially responsible for the current state of the world today and that it wasn't just the fault of the one percent or so of the global human populace with most of the world's material wealth. So it is not simply up to those that we call our masters to change, but we also must change as well.

Though we may not have benefited as much materially as they have, we have contributed to this great big mess. We can, of course, always deny that the social/ecological crises exist and continue demanding that only "they" change, but there is no "us" or "them," only WE.

If we refuse to solve our social crises, we will perish and if we refuse to solve our ecological crises, we will perish. What can we do? We can either bury our heads in the Earth and hope for the best, while either denying that problems exist or acknowledging that they exist and feeling powerless in changing the global outlook, or we can change the way that we perceive the world (think, imagine, act) and search for better ways of perceiving the world/universe that we co-exist/co-inhabit with other beings.

One method of a new perspective of Reality is the concept of Sustainability. It uses current scientific and mathematical models and theories (in addition to ancient ideas from peoples considered to be much more sustainable than ourselves) to describe ideas, concepts, and ways of living that sustainable human societies have had as their basis for many, many, many years. This shift in our consciousness will require us to think in terms of relationships (contextualization) and no longer simply parts (analysis), thus we will have to move from Galilean, Cartesian, and Newtonian thinking (linear, static, mechanistic thinking), which is the basis for modern, traditional Western medicine and every other modern/post-modern system currently in place in our societies. And move to circular, dynamic, systemic, ecological thinking. This means that we have to question all that is currently in place and seek out a new way of living.

There have been many books and articles written about Sustainability that can be read online, in a library, and borrowed from friends, family members, co-workers, and so on. We must recognize and realize that this is a process, an important process that will take many years. It may possibly take another 500 years to restore balance back to the Earth and to our human family as well. Though, we must also remember that the human family is just one of the many families that make up the Earth that we inhabit and we all are interconnected and interrelated in the Web of Life that sustains each of us. As we prepare for the future, here are some thoughts:

"When we try to pick out anything by itself, we find it hitched to everything else in the universe."
–John Muir in *My First Summer in the Sierra* (1911), 27 July 1869; Source: Wikiquote page on John Muir (https://en.wikiquote.org/wiki/John_Muir); License: Attribution-ShareAlike 3.0 Unported (CC BY-SA 3.0)

"A new type of thinking is essential if mankind is to survive and move toward higher levels."
–Albert Einstein in From "Atomic Education Urged by Einstein", *New York Times* (25 May 1946), and later quoted in the article "The Real Problem is in the Hearts of Man" by Michael Amrine, from the *New York Times* Magazine (23 June 1946). A slightly modified version of the 23 June article was reprinted in *Einstein on Peace* by Otto Nathan and Heinz Norden (1960), and it was also reprinted in *Einstein on Politics* by David E. Rowe and Robert Schulmann (2007), p. 383; Source: Wikiquote page on Albert Einstein (https://en.wikiquote.org/wiki/Albert_Einstein); License: Attribution-ShareAlike 3.0 Unported (CC BY-SA 3.0)

Endnotes

[1] The Earth was created approximately 4600 million years ago and the Australopithecus were in existence about 4 million years ago (Lucy belongs to this genus). Therefore, the genus Australopithecus and the resulting descending species have only been on the planet Earth for approximately 0.086956% of the time that the Earth has existed. [4 million years/4600 million years = $8.69565e^{-04}$ and $8.69565e^{-04}$ * 100% = 0.086956%]. (Brandt)

[2] Roughly starting with the voyages of Christopher Columbus (1492 onward), that has been approximately 500 years from the current time. [500 years/4600 million years = $1.0869565e^{-07}$ * 100% = $1.0869565e^{-05}$% ≈ $1.09e^{-05}$% = 0.0000109%].

[3] The next 50 to 100 years. [100 years/4600 million years = $2.173913e^{-08}$ * 100% = $2.173913e^{-06}$% and 50 years/4600 million years = $1.08695652e^{-08}$ * 100% = $1.08695652e^{-06}$%]

The Twilight Zone

http://www.ishmael.org/Education/Parables/SinkingShip.shtml
Sinking Ship

Creating a World That Works for All
Sharif Abdullah

Life in the Barrel

Jason and the Argonauts

Works Cited

Brandt, Niel. Evolutionary and Geological Timelines. The Talk.Origins Archive. 9 Apr. 2004 <http://www.talkorigins.org/origins/geo_timeline.html>.

Originally written in 2004 and posted on "The Crisis in Perception and What We Can Do About It" Web site {http://www.questionuniverse.com/oldway/crisis/crisis_home.html}.

Untitled: Why I Chose Homeopathy

Hello, my name is Irucka Ajani Embry. I've written this letter to the editor of *Health & Wellness* Magazine as I feel that my thoughts can help expand the horizons of interested people within the Central Kentucky area. I've picked this particular publication because it services a widespread area of the Bluegrass, including most of the medical facilities. I hope that my experiences as told through this medium may help others find the strength to educate themselves more about complimentary and alternative systems of healing.

Growing up my parents taught us to look at the whole world in a holistic manner. Thus, I did not view the world as separate, disconnected realities as is prescribed by Western thinking and its institutions, especially medicine. Needless to say, I learned growing up to look at my health holistically too. Therefore, it was not difficult to accept the concepts behind homeopathy and other alternative systems of therapeutic medicine (acupuncture, osteopathy, naturopathy, therapeutic massage, reflexology, etc.).

In 1999, I began seeing a homeopath and since then I have begun to heal and am still in the process of doing so. Homeopathy is based on the Law of Similars ("like cures like"). It is a scientific medical system that cures the whole entire person's being from the inside out using minute doses of a remedy that provides support for our vital force (life energy) that is seen in a physical form as the biochemical defense mechanism. This healing system recognizes that a person's level of health is affected on many

Untitled: Why I Chose Homeopathy

levels from the outermost regions of the Universe to the community in which this person lives. It's not just a matter of taking the remedy and everything will automatically exist within harmony in your body. It will take time, as true healing takes time.

Due to my upbringing, homeopathy, and my own quest for true health, happiness, and wellness, I strive to live the best life that I can in all aspects so that I can live a long, vibrant life.

Once the connection is made between our health and the health of the Earth, it only makes sense that we would become advocates for the Earth as our own well-being depends on her health.

Irucka Ajani Embry
Lexington, KY

Printed in the October 2004 issue of the *Health & Wellness* Magazine.

[Author's Note: The author did not transfer his copyright over to the newspaper so he retains his rights.]

Untitled: 2004 Post Selection Thoughts

I was and was not surprised at the outcome of the selection of the presidential and vice-presidential electors. I had a faint feeling that once again the selection of those electors would be stolen to bring forth the current resident in the White House. Just as Albert Gore, Jr. actually should have been inaugurated as the President, if the electors chose him to be the President, John Kerry should be inaugurated as the President, if the electors chose him to be the President. We need to change our very Constitution and our very ways of electing electors (electoral college, one-day voting during the work/school week, various state laws for the national election, computerized voting, media polls manufacturing the perception of potential voters, and so on). What are we going to do about this 2nd stolen election? Recall the Resident in the White House? Ask for an independent process for impeachment for this Resident's administration, including the Resident? Mobilize and organize ourselves at the grassroots level and continue in the 1st US American Revolution (as the so-called Revolutionary War that ended in 1783 was not a true revolution in any way)?

The outcome means the same for the peace and environment community as did the aftermath of the 2000 selection process.

In order to better educate ourselves, we must free ourselves of the Crisis in Perception. Number one, there is no such thing as the "environment." We, as human beings, are made of the Earth. Thus, we are part of the Earth and the Earth exists all around us.

Untitled: 2004 Post Selection Thoughts

There is no separation. Security is not the security of one separate place around the world, but it is a global security that we should be after. That is where peace manifests from. Back to the question about how do we educate ourselves and others; it will be a matter of redefining education and redefining how we define ourselves as human beings too. We will have to reach the core of our beliefs and start transformations there.

How do we reach those US Americans that voted primarily on "moral" values? That's a good question. First, let's define those "moral" values. Are racism/ethnocentrism, homophobia, sexism, and other forms of discrimination "moral" values? Are fear and hatred "moral" values? Are violence/murder/war/terrorism "moral" values? Is the "Republicrat" Party (Republicans = Democrats at the source) based on those ideals? What would Jesus think about US foreign and domestic policy?

Overall, we must recognize that we have a Crisis in Perception that we must see through. For more information, check out http://www.questionuniverse.com/oldway/newthing.html and the various links to other Web pages.

Where do we go from here? What are you going to do? What are we going to do?

Thank-you all.

The thoughts above were posted online at the following

inactive link: http://www.demaction.org/dia/organizations/2020vision/comments.jsp?blog_entry_KEY=181
Thoughts on the Elections on November 04, 2004:

Were you surprised about the election outcome? What do you think the outcome means for the environment and peace community? What do we need to better educate voters on environment and security issues? How do we reach Americans who said they voted primarily based on moral values? (Go to http://www.washingtonpost.com/wp-dyn/articles/A23700-2004Nov3.html to read reflections from the *Washington Post*)

Untitled: Who am I?

Who am I?
I am who?
Who am I?
¿Quién soy?
¿Soy quién?
¿I am who? ☺
Crazy, insane, liar, thief, former assassin, violently re- & o-pressive, mean, frightening, nervously twitchy, bringer of suffering, taker
Compromiser, Guardian, Friend, Helper/Assistant, Patient & wise disciple/priest/student/teacher, Disciple, Priest, Court Jester, Student, Teacher, Teacher/Student, King, Heretic/Healer, Charmer, Hopeful in Excellence, Change Agent, *the Questioner*, Universes Studier/Inquirer, Dreamer, Creative Imaginer, Thinker, Artist, Musician, Cook/Chef, Photographer, Truth Teller Seeking..., Forgiver, SPIRITUAL BEING ☺, Giver, Recorder, Believer, Lover, Sensualist, Massager, Gardener/Farmer, Familial Member
Former self-imaged & described schizophrenic
Former self-Hater
        Speaker of gibberish
        Werewolf
        Angry Black man
        Mean & Hateful
        Lazy
        Pig – literal & figurative gluttonous child/young man/boy

Untitled: Who am I?

Hater of the US
Racist
Sexist
Thin/skinny
Strange
Idiot
Over-thinker
Over-achiever
Evil if non-Christian
Corruptor
Destroyer
Unknown
Non/unconformist
Nappy Headed
Bad hair
Uncombed
Fool
Why does he act that way?
Why does he do what he does?
Uncontrollable
Nonunderstandable
Indescribable
Criminal
Hater
Different
Too sensitive -- overly
Outsider
Biased
Ugly
          Disrespectful

Untitled: Who am I?

Do U feel that eYe can be described in such a way?
Do U feel that I have grown or have the ability to improve?
Do U feel that Uoy really wonK Me?
Have U tried to Understand ME?
Have eYe tried to understand thee?
What makes Him who He is?

I felt that this poem would be way too personal to include in the 1st collection or anthology. I'll take my time in describing my TRUE Selves in a manner as to allow a mirror for my Soul. Who knows one day I may be able to truly open up the rest of my Soul.

On suicide
I used to be & feel suicidal
My vital force was low
I was afraid of what I would become
I did Not want to FA$_c$E THE MiЯROR of My Past
Now I know that suicide is not, I repeat, **NOT** an option!! In this free-versal poetic reflection, I, Irucka Ajani Embry, declare that I will NOT attempt Nor commit suicide for any reason. If "news" reports declare that I have committed suicide, then do not believe the hype -- the lies that have been put forward to Hide what really happened to this Being. No matter what is done to this Being, a change shall still come. The many diverse seeds have already been sowed and will grow in time.

        Sad
        Frowner
        Hurtful
        Mean-spirited

Untitled: Who am I?

    Won't make it
    Absolved from Reality
Is this Me too?

Beautiful smiler
Deep thinker
Problem preventer/solver
Specially gifted
Enchanter
Eccentric
Knowledgeable
Wise
Old man
Young man
Being
Life Form
Human Being
Star
Child
Creative thinker
Hopeful in a True 1st US American REVOLUTION
Believer in another way -- there has to be another way --
ALTERNATIVES
There are other possibilities - WE must bring them out of our Dream Worlds & Bring them into our Awoken World!! ☺
Change Agent
Revolutionary Activist Seeker
Exceller
Peace Lover
LifeWisher

Untitled: Who am I?

Affirmer
Answer Seeker
Sun/solar (star)   L
Moon   O
Stars   V
Planetary alignment   E
Mother Earth   R
Unifier
Beautiful
Pretty
Spiritual
Hairy
Complementer
Educator
Friendly smile
Laugher
Child-like (WE are all the child of SOMEone ☺ }
Thankful
Learner
Survivor/Recoverer
Overturner
ReDefiner
Searcher
Crier
Story-teller
Finder
Questioning: Who are thou? Thou art who?
Discover of ThySelf
Self-improver
Researcher

Untitled: Who am I?

Singer
Documenter
Reconnector
Joiner
Realizer
US American (People in the Western Hemisphere belong to North or South America in modern colonialist/imperialist terminology)
Roots? Where am I from?

For those that may have heard this particular poem before in person: I have allowed these thoughts to settle & mature before placing them in a written form. None the less the original spirit is still here: the intent to search within. I hope that what I have developed in this form will assist you in your own Journeys.

Journeyer
Contextualist
Former Analyzer/Analyst
Emotionally Stabilizing
Seeking the SOURCE

I recognize that this poem is not exactly what I planned it to be or representative of what most of us have come to believe is representative of poetry: Oh well, 'tis Life.

I am who I am.
I am I am who.
I am, I am, who.
I am who I am.

Untitled: Who am I?

I am a former believer of biological "identification" marker: race.
I am who I have chosen to be.
I am following my Fate.
I am on my Path.
I am doing what the Higher Beings have allowed me to Be & do.
I am becoming Selfish (notice the Big "S" in Selfish -- it is the Larger conception of myself) as compared to my former selfish self. Thank-you Mohandas K. Gandhi (the Mahatma) for your giving of so much to the world. Thank-you ALL -- to EVERYone else in the world for the guidance.

Meaningful
        Ecstatic

I am more than what I seem.
Look at what I mean.
Look into my eyes & see what I've seen.
I know that we have a long way to go.
We must find the better Ways.
I know that I must start here with ME.
If I don't, then I'm only kidding mySelf.
I must be Real to mySelf.
I must be Forgiving of mySelf.
I must know ThySelf.
I MUST LOVE ☺ MySelf.
I MUST Remember.
I MUST be Present at all times.
I must massage myself into wellness with Homeopathy as my Guiding Light.
I must sow organic & biodynamic seeds in the Gardens of the

Untitled: Who am I?

Earth -- Life! ☺
I must ReKnow my tongues.
I must Reaffirm my place alongside that of those whose paths will converge to continue this Healing process.
"Stop talking about it & BE about it!"
What gets done is what you have done.
Be prayerful at all times.
We are truly Blessed.

Non-alcoholic drinker
Interesting
Spiritually Science Driven
Nonconformist, yet Conformist to Nonconformity (Thank-you H ...).
Football
Fútbol
Soccer
Lover of games
Lover of fun
Lover of family
Medicine

Where are WE going?
Where are WE?
Where Have WE been?
¿Science or Religion or Science & Spirituality?
Place-based
Advisor
Receiver

Untitled: Who am I?

These are only single-dimensional partial Realities pre-supposed and based upon the actions/actions, thoughts, feelings, problems of this particular individual known as Irucka Ajani Embry. However, as an inhabitant of a multi-dimensional world, these concepts can not accurately or fully describe or designate this being. Thus, only use what I have written as a guide or tool in attempting to understand this particular systemic set of waves/particles enhanced in this time, place, and spatial dimensional realizations. Thank-U.

##

Jus' let the Muses (Greek mythology) guide U: How can a Being who once assassinated, executed, murdered & raped/tortured other beings for $, fame, love of Fear, power, notoriety, powerlessness, insecure feelings, self-hatred & hatred of all other Genus/Species related Kingdom Beings [Notice the masculine regalness apparent in this biological classification}, a way to avoid commitment, and due to a programmed overly negative outLook on Life☹ (Let us not forget hunter) speak of Conscience & Conscientious Objection to the acts of suicide, murder, rape, torture, depopulating [depeopling], ecological (environmental, social, political, economic, legal/judicial, terrestrial/Earthly, Universals) destruction, financial scams, weapons research & manufacturing & sales, cosmic negative disturbances emanating as waves/particles/super strings (Quantum & Super Strings Theories], Divide & Conquer on Behalf of so-called global elites & New World Order & Illuminati & Reptilians (Reptile + Human = R-Complex) & world conquering

Untitled: Who am I?

Extra-Terrestrials (YES, Aliens do Exist -- they have visited & lived here on Earth for thousands or millions or billions of years}, drugging through use of [antibiotics, vaccines, suppressive drugs, chemical gas agents, radiochemical Depleted Uranium, napalm, chemical liquid/solid molecular agents, FEAR = TERRORISM = Stress = Negativity = Dictatorships = "Democracy" or "Republic" or "Socialist"/"Communist" or military junta or non-military Dictatorship, biological gas/liquid/solid agents, electromagnetic (over)dose, radiological gas/liquid/solid agents, biotelemetric chips, etc.], drug & petroleum smuggling to hide worldwide economic depressions & recessions & downfalls by virtue of the failed United States of America petrodollar & the worldwide economic/financial systems intertwined with "illegal" drug money Wall$treet, spiritual emptiness & starving -- as I am still recovering from imperial/capitalist/"socialist"/"communist" schemes of mind/body/spirit control & domination over the world's peoples & falsely reality currency economically profit-driven spoils that is ☹ WAR!!☹ ☹ ☹ ?

I, Irucka Ajani Embry, am a Conscientious Objector to War. I am a citizen of the United States of America & the Earth. I object to War just as I object to the death penalty in all forms practiced today. I object to the US "corporament's" manipulation of the people of the world in its quest on behalf of the so-called global elites to Commit War against the world. I object to blind patriotism (patriarchy, the "Fatherland," masculinity) & nationalism. [I am a Being/Life Form & then an Animal & then a Human Being & then a Male. I am Not against males nor females. I am for Balance & the return to the cycle of matriarchy (femininity, the Motherland, matriarchy) to Balance with the

Untitled: Who am I?

over-extended stay of patriarchy, which has put the world in a major imbalance. Study & understand the wisdom of the Earth's Indigenous Peoples to learn more.] I object to the objectification & dehumanization that "the people behind the uniforms" are subjected to & subject the peoples that they objectify & dehumanize on behalf of their (blind) allegiance & patriotism & inability to think/act in one's truest conscience due to their training. I object to their objectification & dehumanization because it directly and/or indirectly objectifies & dehumanizes each & every one of us. We ALL live on this planet & must not allow us to destroy ourselves. I support "the people behind the uniforms" (see the discussion below):

20 December 2004
15 March 2005

Untitled: Religion ≠ Spirituality

PraYers & LibatiOns ☺ For The Dearly Departed
Thank-you to ALL of the AncestorS for bringing Us into Being!
Present
 Thank-U to ALl who are sowing seeds of reBirth, reClaiming, creatiVity, Peace, Love ☺, Understanding, ReSpect, Inclusivity, & Life!!
Future
 Thank-you for entrusting Us to bring U into Being!! ☺

Religion ≠ Spirituality
 Religion is a socio-cultural (social/societal cultural) institution based on separation [womyn from man & man from womyn -- femininity from masculinity -N- masculinity from femininity and society from Nature (whereas Nature or the Earth is seen as feminine or the dimension/domain/realm/world of pagans & healers & heathens & non-believers & Hell-bound lost souls & "scantily-clad uncivilized tribes" that need to be "civilized" to know God assisted by missionaries through the help of the Gun, Sword, torture chamber(s), illusory moneyed/currency economic system(s), and terrorism}].
Spirituality is the way 1 lives their Life each and every conscious & unconscious moment of each & every day. Spirituality is based on Inclusivity. Spirituality is the Essence of the Spirit. We believe

Untitled: Religion ≠ Spirituality

that at one juncture of the time-space fabric (continuum] that Religion =ed Spirituality; however, there was a chasm. Religion changed its path & course. On the other hand, Spirituality stayed on its continuum.

*E*xceptionalism
        Religious people are perfectly saved so they will enter Heaven/Paradise regardless of what they think, feel, do, or don't do. If you are not religious (in the good ol' USA -- not Christian], then you are not a good person since you are not perfectly saved. The same is for religious societies

(Note: The concept of Religion is often used, misused, and abused by the people that consider themselves to be wealthy & elite in societies throughout the Story of the world. The practice of the "same" religion varies throughout time-space due to socio-cultural traditions, beliefs, customs, & influences. Religion is shaped by the forces bringing about this institution in a particular place at a juncture of the time-space fabric.}:

The USA "corporament" (corporate = government) commits atrocious crimes at home, yet is considered to be Perfect abroad because this is a Christian society (or at least that's what we're told}.

The atrocious crimes:
— the witch hunts for [alleged heretics], healers, empowered & strong womyn, Truth Seekers "out-of-the-box"

— the Holy Wars (? - go figure -- There's holiness in the orgy

Untitled: Religion ≠ Spirituality

blood bath of War]

— the ecologicAl Crisis

— colonialism, capitalism, corporate globalization, & imperialism

— missionary-based schools

— enslavement

— Manifest Destiny

— the use of the military to terminate strikes of people who dared to form a union

— the practice of scalping (how much for a child? how much for a man? how much for a womyn?}

— the rape, torture, and exploitation of people incarcerated in jails & prisons by people allegedly there to "protect" the people incarcerated (Note: people = men & womyn in each use of the word}

— the continued use of Capital Punishment & vengeance to allegedly solve problems (read: kill people) -- How can people speak about the Right to Life, yet not speak out loudly against Capital Punishment? [once again, go figure?) Didn't the religious figures speak about forgiveness, "turning the other cheek," and Restorative Justice? Wasn't the Sun of God in Christian theology, Jesus Christ (to those who speak English - - whether English was forcibly taught or not], killed/executed by Capital Punishment? Does the constant display of the "Holy Cross" reinforce the ideas of violence & Capital Punishment {Thank-you KRS-One for that inspiration to address said question)?

If the Ten Commandments forbade murder, then why does Capital Punishment & aggressive/defensive Wars [that is state-sanctioned murder in Capital Punishment by the executioners -- including the police and other state actors -- and state-sanctioned murder & suicide in War) still persist in Christendom?

— the distortion & lie-filled books, especially history books

— Michelangelo painting the image(s) of the Sun of God in Christian theology   Jesus Christ -- as an Anglo-Saxon male in the Sistine Chapel over the previous image(s) of Jesus Christ. This was done before Europe sought to invade, conquer, violate, rape, pillage, "civilize," and exploit the rest of the World. The image(s) pained by Michelangelo did not match the descriptions in *The Holy Bible* of Jesus Christ (n)or those images of Jesus Christ from earlier ages in Europe & Africa & Asia(?).

Why was Michelangelo commissioned to re-interpret the image of Jesus Christ? Who was/were the commissioner(s)? Why did Europe change its view towards the rest of the world, i.e. What socio-economic-political forces were at play?

Was everyone in Europe accepting of this attitude change? If so, why? If not, why not? Who resisted? Who accepted?

Untitled: Religion ≠ Spirituality

This reconfiguring of the Sun of God to an European male (modern day Caucasian/white male in our conception of "race" sense] has had profound affects & effects over the centuries.

— the end of mysticism & magic or their marginalization or a mixture of both

— the conception of marriage as a property relationship where sexual intercourse can only take course as long as the purpose is procreation (reproduction) ONLY.☹

Of course, the only possible position is where the man is in control with his power on top of the woman - - the missionary position. Therefore any sexual drive or libido or interest is cast down upon.

Do you own your wife?
Do U want to own your wife?
Can all parties to the contractual relationship of marriage file for a divorce? If not, why not?
Can all religious leaders or followers marry? If not, why not?
Do you enJoy sex?

Marriage has been denied to "property" -- classified as 3/5ths (three-fifths) of a human being with the one-drop rule -- with other "property." [¡EyE Do NOT view my ancestors as "property!" I've only used that term here to make this point.]

Marriage has been denied to people formerly viewed as

Untitled: Religion ≠ Spirituality

"property" with those people that had been viewed as second-class citizens. Marriage has been denied to people of the same sex.

Why?

If this is the "free" world, then shouldn't people have the right to marry? Why is/has the right to marry been denied?

If womyn have to (who decides? Why?) dress modestly & cover most of their body, then shouldn't men act accordingly? Does this have anything to do with male sexual urges, impulses, drives, libidos, and (lack of} self-control have anything to do with those modalities?

How can We reconceptualize the idea & institution of marriage?

Don't breastfeed your child(ren) in public, better yet, don't breastfeed your child(ren) at all. Feed them chemical mixtures minus the connective bond to the mother & her immunity instead of breast milk.

Tell the people to be fearful & shameful of their Naked bodies. Do Not Love ☺ Urself. Therefore be fearful & shameful of God as we were made by God in the image of God.

Is this the Reality of Religion & Marriage?

— Thanksgiving Holiday (the Myth)
        Puritans not Pilgrims

Untitled: Religion ≠ Spirituality

Thank-ful to God for the extermination of the indigenous peoples & the food they shared (their buried physical bodies, their buried foods, & their knowledge of edible/inedible foods in the area}

— the legacy of Christopher Columbus
God, gold, and glory through the display of the "exotic" peoples in Europe & their enslavement & their tortured rape/exploitation/executions & their change from "uncivilized" to "civilized" people

Note: I use the word: "uncivilized," "civilized," "exotic," & "tribe"/"tribal" to make various points about the use of language through written words and their associated imagery & symbolism. I do Not share those views.

Note: Judaism gave birth to Christianity and then Christianity gave birth to Islam. The various points above refer to the 3 major modern-day religions of the world. Thus, the atrocious crimes are Not **all** attributable to the USA. However, the USA is a product of that continuum of history & in some ways reinforces & rebirths concepts that have not been in widespread practice in the modern world. In actuality, the USA is like any other product of human intention, good, bad, a mixture of good & bad, and in-between good & bad.

<u>L</u>ove
        Love God.
        Love your friends & enemies.
        Love Urself, what about your naked body?

Untitled: Religion ≠ Spirituality

Love your neighbors.
Do not love the Earth & all of her children. Be stewards of and/or dominate Ur relatives.

Love is the reason why I have this (com)passion & compulsion to pen this poetic fluctuation of versal unrhythmic titillations of epic & free verse poetic mastery, illusory, enigma, and mystery. Spiritual people are Not perfect. Religious people are Not perfect. Non-spiritual & Non-religious people are Not perfect. I am Not perfect. We are Not perfect.

We have a narrative to share about Religion & War:

I love God. (Now that I really think about it, I fear God & the wrath of God if I did not Love God.] I love my country since we're always told of our great Christian traditions that we must share (force) with the rest of the world. {Once again, I would say that after thinking, I feared the wrath of my country & her patriotically enthused & infused inhabitants.] It was that Love that led me to the recruiter's office. The office was located in a community populated by people that were economically (read: material wealth] disempowered & marginalized & were blessed with permanent & temporary suntans.

We, the people, were told by the "corporament" complex that the "enemy(ies)" who attacked this perfectly gentle nation-state was/were outside our borders. (By the way, with all of the stolen lands all over the world, where do the boundaries really exist?}

Untitled: Religion ≠ Spirituality

I was enraged. Even though God seeks justice, not revenge, the religious officials supported the call to arms. If they approved of this cause & I loved God & my country, then what was I waiting for? I had a high school diploma, yet I could not find a job. I couldn't afford to attend a college or university. I had nothing left to lose, since I had nothing. No, I had something:

—video games displaying the ease of War

—years of being picked on by my peers, 'cause I did "turn the other cheek" as I had been taught through "the Good Book"

—intense patriotic feelings for God & my country. I was a Christian & so was my country.

—the drive to want to drive and/or ride in a military-issue Hummer

—pictures of returning troops & the celebratory crowds

—God Bless the USA stickers (what about everyone else?)

—the need to belong & feel altruistic (the need to conform to the dictates of authority figures -- preacher/Minister/priest/Deacon/Pastor/Reverend, teachers, parents, government "leaders" in my Life}.

—intense pride in a history full of distortions, deletions, & outright lies

Untitled: Religion ≠ Spirituality

—the need to impress a woman I had a crush on who enjoyed the company of men in uniforms

—and lastly the need to follow with nothing of something or something of nothing, I enlisted in the USA military. I won't bore you with all of the details.

One day we were asked {screamed at in a demeaning, loud mannered voice):

"What makes the grass grow?!!!!"

Everyone, except me, knew the correct response: "BLOOD makes the grass grow!!"

I couldn't believe my ears, BLOOD makes the grass grow!? By this time I had forgotten all about the omnipotently present outside "enemy." I was only concerned about trying to keep up with my unit. Weren't we fighting for democracy & freedom for our "enemies?" Weren't we a Christian nation fighting to spread Love & defend ourselves against an outside attacker? What did all of this have to do with blood & the grass growing?

I started shivering & crying. The Drill Sergeant saw me & told me that I was a sissy and a girl. He informed me that even the females participated fully in this exercise. He admonished me & said that I should take my "gay ass" home if I would not follow his rules set down by Uncle Sam. I ran out of place in line, still crying

Untitled: Religion ≠ Spirituality

& shivering, & looked for the Chaplain's Office. I heard the Drill Sergeant give the order to jeer me. I made it to the Chaplain's Office full of tears in my Is. I spoke to the Chaplain about my ordeal that day.

The Chaplain asked me if I was gay since I was crying. He also admonished me for not following orders for he saw nothing wrong with it. The Chaplain said joyously: "BLOOD makes the grass grow!!" He repeated that phrase over & over again. Though I had stopped crying temporarily, I began to cry again. The Chaplain scolded me by saying that only gay men cry & that God does not like gay men. Therefore I could not cry nor be a gay men nor fight in God's military. I immediately stopped crying & toughened up myself so that I could "act like a real man."

The Chaplain asked me if I wanted to see his "trophy" from a previous "defensive" War effort. I nodded in agreement.

18 April 2005

Volume 3: The Great Years: 2005–2014

Untitled: Celebratory Uncles in tha mornin' dew of Life

It all started with Unc
        Uncle J B
then it was Uncle A
        Uncle A B
then Uncle L
        Uncle L M
Uncle A left years later
        Uncle A H
Uncle D a few feathers of time beyond Uncle A
        Uncle M D

Now ☺ ☹: (?)

It seems that we must celebrate yet anotha'
        Uncle
        Father-figure
        Father/Dad/Daddy
        Brother
        Cousin
        Husband
        Son/Son-in-law
        Friend
        Confidant
        Nephew
        Neighbor

Untitled: Celebratory Uncles in tha ...

    Leader
    Male Being

Celebrate what?!? - - in this time of Remembrance, Reflective Memory Recall for Collection, Grieving, Crying, Praying, Meditating, Traveling, Singing, Asking, Wondering, Not Believing, Spreading Love ...

Celebrate what we have Received from having been touch (physically, mentally/intellectually, emotionally, & spiritually) by the Earthly presence of those Men that I have been privileged to Call my
    Uncles
    Father-figures
    Educators
Although they are no longer physically with us, they will always be with us
    in the pictures we took
    in the stories told
    in the lessons given & learned
    in the fishing trips
    in the conversations
    in the games played & watched
    in the laughter shared
    in the joy we share with other family & friends [loved ones!! ☺ }
    in the joy of knowing their presence
    in the garages housing the ideas, laughter, food, and

ALL that we shared
>> in the sports anecdotes
>> in the people (famous & not so famous) we met &
shared great times with through our great connector(s)
>> in the discipline & examples handed down
>> in the work ethic
>> in the love of family & friends
>> in the LOVE OF LIFE!!

Since they are not with us Here & Now
>> I want to personally THANK ALL of my Uncles that have left this plane of existence for being who they were.

THANK-YOU ALL

Although I may not have wanted to hear all that any One of U had to say at that time, I want to say that I appreciate the Time that you set aside to Guide Me and/or my Twin Brother.
I hope that I am able to show Each of U the lessons taught that I have learned.

I'm writing this stream of consciousness in College Park, Maryland, as I'm here along with other family to Celebrate yet anotha Uncle & His Life:
Uncle R W E as he prepares to turn 60 (Sixty) years of age in a couple of days.

I was torn about whether to mourn with family on the future

Untitled: Celebratory Uncles in tha ...

passing of Uncle V from his Earthly vessel to the next level of Life -- Heaven, the Other Side -- by celebrating His Life & Gifts to Each of US

OR

Whether to Celebrate Uncle R in his 6 Decade Life.

I chose to
 Both Celebrate the Life of Uncle V & the Life of Uncle R.

Uncle V enjoyed to see people happy & **_eating good_** so I am able to Celebrate his Life by sharing his contagious Spirit of Goodwill with Baba's family up here in the MD.

When I left the ICU room, where Uncle V & Aunt I lay, around 2 or 3 AM after traveling for several hours on the road I told Uncle V that I would see him in the morning.

I will see Uncle V each & every morning as I get up to Live my Life to the fullest extent possible because that is my git to each of my Uncles:
 Returning to the World what they have graciously bestowed upon me & so many others.

I LOVE YOU ALL!! ☺

Let's CELEBRATE LIFE

4 March 2006

Untitled: Climate Strange

Before I opine prosaically impudent words upon Climate Change/Global Warming, I will provide an utterance on

Restrictive dogma on the impossibilities of possibilities in a supra-human animal Universe of Universes
Easily biased by the guiding influences of tha Intelligentsia/Illuminati who have tried to disparage anything that extends beyond the reaches of "Real Science"
w**A**sn't (& Isn't) Eugenics & <u>ALL</u> of its descendants "REal Science"
Let us complete the list: Human-induced [not bacterial-induced} biotechnologies (genetic engineering, cloning, genetically modified organisms, genetically engineered "food," "disease" engineering, the Human Genome Project, stem cell research, etc.}, population control measures designed to alleviate the concern with the human carrying capacity of our Mother Earth

lacking a **S**ystems view of Life in its myriad of interconnections, hidden & manifest, throughout each of the Worlds
be **C**areful to recognize that we have only a limited complete understanding of the Whole of Nature
Insist on being
humbl**E**
k**N**ow that Creativity/Creation is more encompassing than knowledge alone
surely intelligen**C**e is not the end all & be all of our existence in this place at this particular junction of temporal & spatial dimensionality

Untitled: Climate Strange

Expect that human-based biases will inflect scientific processes & that Real Science must include Reality (which can not always be reduced [reductionism} or organized systematically -- systems thinking -- as humans can only comprehend or view what they allow to be perceived & later interpreted in their flat EArth consciousness -- just those that have not elevated their mindset above a level ground datum

Now back to

Global means worldwide, the Whole Earth, Mother Earth, Gaia, international, all 7 continents & the roughly 70% bodies of water, the apparent & obscure worlds, ALl the dimensions, North, South, East, & West therefore global *is not* restricted to on**L**y 1 nation, a group of countries, or particular regions
Of course all aspects of Life are in constant flux
change is inevita**B**le
thus clim**A**te can, has, & will have its transformations too
tha prob**L**ems of the orb are intimately related & interconnected & must be solved as such

Wishing away radical, spiritual science does not make it go away
Awareness
Refuse to be bought & sold by the highest bidder
beco**M**e a whistleblower
thermodynam**I**cs as a component of Global Warming/Climate Change debates
ack**N**owledge Ur funding source {foundations, organizations, individuals, financial institutions, colleges & universities,

Untitled: Climate Strange

"corporament" = corporate + government)
thinkinG beyond: Sacred Geometry, nonlinear dynamics/complexity theory, chaos theory/fractal intelligence, systems thinking, ecological literal thinking, Creativity Consciousness, Peace & Love within

////////

Coming with stronger & more frequent storms
Lurking in the backdrop of the debate: HAARP, cloud seeding, chemtrails, & other methods of altering climates & human states of consciousness
the market Is not the answer, it has greatly exacerbated many of our interrelated quandries
Meet the Earth & thy shall know thy Self
reseArch via the Internet, libraries, journals & magazines, newspapers, television & personal observations & experiences
Tell others
Expect backlash from skeptics with powerful backers

Come to Ur own conclusions
Happiness & laughter in times of opportune impossible possibilities
Act in y(our) best interests
kNow your place & your purpose in this location
act Globally & locally
Encourage others to ask the ?'s that have difficult & challenging answers

Ultimately what we do or don't do is our Choice

Ethnocentric overtones, though aLl encompassing
United against the weak & infirmed
Guided by population control fears
Experiments with humans
Not a relic of the past, continues today
Includes forced sterilizations
Controversial though not widely known
Selective gene pooling for reeding purposes

##

Earth tilts
Carbon dioxide raises the Earth closer to our Star -- **the Sun**
Ice Age or Global Warming?
Non-human focused (volcanic activity, digestive gases expelled by non-human animals, respiration, and so on) or human-focused (greenhouse gases, power plants, lawn mowers, automobiles, "fossil" fuels & non-"fossil" fuels, and so on)?
Geologic time versus human-centered time?
Heat island effects
Hot stormwater runoff
Acid deposition
Air/water/land/terrestrial body pollution
Carbon source or sink?
Microbial factories
False science is lame
Biomimic photosynthesis
Science is God or Science is a Student-Teacher?
Laws are meant to be broken when not absolute.

Untitled: Climate Strange

Our ways are evolving
Aliens-R-Us
Relate this to us All
What do these lines have to do w/ the previous focused indignations of the topic of Science?
"I don't know."

You, the artistic renderer interpreter, must decide what U think about these coniptions.

Space-age conspiracies abound in jumbled thoughts circumnavigating alpha & beta brainwaves in this Earthly vessel prosecting on the Designs of Life.
Some things are trife, others are rife for exploratory enthusiasm.
Blast off to outer space so that we can reDefine our inner space.
Realize the magnitude of yr thoughts on Ur actions.
Remember that Science is Everywhere.

Spellbound yourself for a tale.

Represent in the Universal Game of Life.

Know the movies of your <u>piece</u>.

Peace is a corollary function of the mind feeding off of Love.

Love is Pure Energy indeed.

All Life is Pure Energy indeed.

Untitled: Climate Strange

Subatomic particles to waves to super strings.

Entropy at its best is organized confusive conscriptions.

Play it safe.

Safe food for everyone (Real Food just tastes better].

A soldier of fortune is still a mercenary.

Don't we all have national mercenary forces?

The "People Behind the Uniforms" must unbecome their conditioning.

The People United in Love can overcome our dictatorial rulers.

Our rulers can not contort our Science, Politics, and Religious Spiritualities 4-Ever.
We'll Wake-Up soon enough or it'll be too late.

Leave the conspirators at the door & enter w/ your hidden 3rd Eye.

Don't sign your Life over to their Way of Life.

The elites have divided us, but not yet conquered us.

They must not vanquish our Spirits.

Untitled: Climate Strange

Spirit is Pure Energy.

Pure Energy is Breath.

Breath is LIfe.

Life is Love.

Life is Good.

Good is Energy.

We must seek inner to heal the outer.

Food is a wise medicine.

Medicine is only a tool, not the Way.

Health is a Way.

Eugenics for master breeding of the elite bloodlines. Royalty incestuous relations are not the only. Follow the bloodlines & tha money.

Money is an illusion. Credit is a bigger illusion.

Gift the Economy.

Free Software 4 all.

Untitled: Climate Strange

Cocaine residue falling from tha sky in a state of emergency.

Continuity of Government (COG) since WW II & still operates today.

Nuclear power whereas the reactor is millions of miles away is a free energy source.

Authenticate U. Be freely responsible.

Forgiveness is a Divine Act.

There are many facets of Science booming out of your booming creatively mental Spiritual appliance.

Monday, 5 June 2006
5 July 2008

Untitled: Prosaically delineating fortuitous gifts of virtue in a familial tonality

I'm writing this poem (creative collective of abstract prose -- in this instance] as a GifT to not only this Family ☺, but to All families around the globe that can gleam something of significance from these random, yet not so random realizations.

I hope that each of U appreciate an aspect of this gift.

Why?

Much has been given to mE over many years so I feel that it is <u>necessary</u> for mE to give back.

Thank-U aLl for the Past-Present-& tha Future that we collectively created & still shall bring forth into being.

Fun, fulfillment, fantastic,
              funk, fill voids, fragile, frugal,
                          farm(land), farm{work], farm[fresh),
                          farmer's markets,
Fall/Winter/Spring/Summer occasions & festivities
                                    ☺ FOOd ☺ that uplifts
y(OuR) *SpiriTs*
Alleviate stress, fatigue, pains, pangs, and other ailments thru therapies that do Not suppress the body's inherent ability to intuitively HeaL & cuRe
Make time to spend with Urself to reflect, ponder, think, dream,

imagine, create, rElax, reCharge & of course Make time to spend with loved & cherished ones
Isn't it time that we do away with all of the family secrets & allow the youth (us) to become the informed & responsible leaders that we need to & must be?
Let go -- Do U want to be Right or Happy?
allow Yurself & thus the Family Unit(y) to Heal -- Be patient, respectful, and understanding

Have essential fatty acids (EFAs), especially omega-3 {polyunsaturated fats] on a daily basis in > proportion than omega-6 [polyunsaturated fatty acids}
rEalize that health is more than the absence of "dis-ease" on the spiritual/mental/intellectual, emotional/psychic, and/or physical/sexual planes of the human body (spiritual, emotional, & physical aspects & levels]
there are Alternatives for the treatment of cancer symptoms & any other symptomatology that Ur particular being possesses at any particular instance of the intersections of time, space, and place (essentially the best healthcare recognizes that each being -- in this case human -- needs an individualized path to healing & eventually curing}
Listen & love deeply & continuously
it's OK to: eaT healthy foods 4 U
*read the labels of what U eat, smell, taste, drink, wear, & use in any other way
+grow & eat biodynamic &/or organic foods
+use organic &/or biodynamic products
*seek assistance in our continual quest for liberation
*be thankful, joyful, & happy

Untitled: Prosaically delineating ...

*express Ur emotions
+be U, i.e. human -- imperfect
+make exercise enjoyable & part of Ur healthy lifestyle
*ask 4 a 2nd, 3rd, or 4th opinion
= 4 give Urself & others
+understand that organic foods are not *new* [prior to the so-called "Green Revolution" most, if not all, small-scale, non-mono/cash crop farms & gardens employed organic methods}
*believe what U believe
+be Quiet & revel in our connections to Nature 4 we are a part of, not separate, from Nature
*be Wrong & ask for forgiveness
= not have an answer -- simply say eYe do Not knOw
+strengthen Ur 3rd I
= fulfill y(oUr) purpose in this Life
it's okay to love onseLf unconditionally so tHat U truly know U & can recognize the embedded healing & curing aspects & properties buried with-in U & Eye (all of us]

fAmily in all of its forms is important
Now is the time = present
Do today, if possible

Wish 4 significance instead of merely success
crEate family partnerships that strengthen our bonds & broaden familial assets
wealth is not solely material, for it is also immaterial/spirituAl
Learn from past mistakes
Touch the lives of others in a positive way
"tHere's always room for one more"

Untitled: Prosaically delineating ...

Family Health & Wealth was also written, in part, as a response to the deaths of so many men over the past year or so.

We, men & future men, need to get our acts together starting with our very selves.

It's up to each of us.

20 August 2006

Rosacreatius

1 - R o s e is lost & lonely
Two Roses are cozy & found
Too intertwined Roses are cuddly, cozy & found

6 January 2007

Untitled: Apologetically Urse

Ask for forgiveness from the heart
Prepare to be humble & let go
Oh! How human we are indeed!
Lonely tears need a comforting should to cry on
Only U can be responsible for what U did, did not do, said, and/or did not say (the same for I}
Good to be your friend ☺ ☺
You and I

Selfishness overrides better intentions
Ouch! That hurt U & me!
Really need to transform into the better half
Ready to accept responsibility
Yes, it was my fault.

-Master thySelf & learn a new way to approach life's rough spots as they arise
-Look at obstacles as an opportunity for personal growth and fulfillment
-Reach for the stars and you will truly be significant
-Ask: Do I want to be right or happy:?
-What is your purpose & vision? (i.e. Why are YOU here?? ☺]
-Will your past lives help or hinder your evolution?
-How can we learn to forgive, embrace, and support instead of tearing down & ripping apart each other?
-What lessons have you learned?
-What lessons will be tautily understood by you?

Untitled: Apologetically Urse

-Learn to secure the insecurities located within.
-Laugh often and well.
-Speak to and with someone, not @ someone.
-Love thySelf unconditionally.
-Love and live fully.
-Forgiveness is **_Divine_**.
-Imperfectuous human people-induced elements err.
-Step into someone else's existence to understand comprehensively.
-Look deep inside.
-Ensure personal & relational happiness.
-Remember it's the differences that unite us & the similarities that bind us.
-No one is an island existing in an extravagant vacuum devoid of all form, structure, and substance.
-Keep it real, yet tactful.
-Allow love to coalesce and gel, thus taking form.
-Appreciate everyone's uniqueness.
-Face-to-face communication.
-Speak from the heart.
-Open your I's to see and embrace that which is beyond your grasp – confounds & dumbfounds.
-Apologetically sorry I remain.
Purpose
Ease of mind through your heart & whole body
Always remember to live & be peace & not simply speak & do peace
Easier said than done

PEACE = FORGIVENESS

FORGIVENESS = PEACE

Will you be at peace too?

Peace is a state of mind.

Peace comes from the inside out.

Let peace rise in your being.

Allow peace to thrive.

Let go of the past – be in the PreSent.

Be forgiving & peaceful to all parties.

☺ S ☺

                      ☺ M

                                      I ☺

                    ☺ L

E ☺ !!

Untitled: Apologetically Urse

6 January 2007

Momentous Musings in an Opinely Fabulent E-scale flatly G

Melodious
Utterings
Synergistically
Increasing
Creativity

Liberty
In
Fully engaged responsibility
Effectiveness of networked symbiotic syngergisms

Laughter
cOnnective sharings of circular attractive repulsions pulsating
Voluptuously
Evolving through a musikal resonance of frequent clouds of opportunity

Ceasing only to flow into another harmonious pathway of least resistance as a cascading waterfall passes into a wildly rushing river of consciousness
Reaching within, out, beyond, behind, forward, diagonal, side-to-side, sideways, abstractly, yet concretely
Excellence (nuff said ☺]
Actively nonacting
Tactilely explicit in an implicit casualty of significance over success
Invoking a libatious call to the ancestors, children of today, and

Momentous Musings in an Opinely ...

those children yet to arrive {we ARE aLl children)
Vociferous volatilimous vascular vantage
Every being creates & is created – It is our birthright to be creative

Source of Life
Understand ye not fully
Now there is an idea

Move the two molecules hydrogenically bonded to one molecule within us all
Observe with every fiber of Ur being
Optically opaque keen sensitivity
New emergence from a designated process from meaningful formulas chaotically ordered systematically fruitful is a matter of fact

19 April 2007

Nucleated residues isotopically inundated in ounces of bullshit

New materials with extreme half-lives created daily
Understand what we are doing to US?☹
Clearly there must be other options to generate energy – the Sun is the source of all terrestrial energy anyways
Lie to the people, especially those most nearly & directly impacted, about the potential dangers
Even this public relations nightmare is spun out of control
Agreements of non-proliferation don't mean shit
Read about the inherent dangers of this fascination with low-level & high-level radioactive isotopes & speak out for saner technologies, policies, scientists/designers/engineers, energy options & ultimately disposal options for the mess we've already created & subsidized

No más – shall we, the scientists & engineers, renounce radioactive power generation & weapons design (including, but not limited to, electronic, chemical, biological, genetic/genomic, psychological, nuclear, radiological)? ☺]
Our future depends on how we respond collectively to our unparalleled mistakes & misguided designs

—

Now, how do we safely, over geologic time, dispose of the past, present & future wastes?
Oh yeah – lest me not forget the many people that were/are

Nucleated residues isotopically ...

routinely directly (and indirectly) insulted & malignantly treated by having to mine for radioactive materials, live next to or in the vicinity of nucleated sources, transport and store the radioactive materials, carry the scars of past generations for the future to know their sacrifices (whether voluntary or involuntary), breathe the particulate matter, be subjected to for medical treatment and/or experiments, vaporized or burned by nuclear materials, had a bomb detonated or dropped on or nearby you, suffer the indignation of the constant lies & false statements by the technocrats, etc.

It is high noon on the nuclear age, we must find our way back into the light

19 April 2007

Letting all the fucking juices hang out

Serendipitiously secreting olfactory notional pheromones
Erogenous zones tintillating eruptiously
Xuberance
Understanding the connective webs
Actually enjoy it
Loving the spiritual bliss
In the moment
Teasing increases the primal animalistic instincts (yes, we are animals ☺ }
Yes, time apart can pull us closer together

Insist on giving Ur all
Need to continue sexual education

Gotta love the juices flowing & partaken with deep breaths
Orgasmic Reality
Orgasms can be multiplicitous
Dangerous STIs/STDs need not scare U nor eYe – get tested, educate Urself, use protective wisdom & common intuitive sense, love Urself, be honest, share with each other, give & receive so as to be Selfish for the Good

Touch those toes with soft majestic hands oiled up with the finest one ingredient, organic, first cold-pressed moisturizing oils
Insist on knowing Urself first & exploratory techniques
Make-Up sex is great!! ☺
Erotically fantasizing creative imaginative responses holding

Letting all the fucking juices hang out

onto the seen, yet unseen connections
Speak of sexual health {which is only one aspect of a being's overall health]

Intrinsically
Syntaxically sublime sensuality

Liquidous
Omnipresence
Virtually
Everywhere

Exhibiting the unquantifiable qualities of fluidous movement within the genome webbing spiders in circular, nonlinear dynamical fluctuations of flux beyond simplified time-space-place continuums

20 April 2007

Untitled: Controlled thoughts of random interactions aka What tha Fuck Was he Thinkin' Writing this Shit!

Gardens everywhere
Studying permaculture
Eating locally grown biodynamic and/or organic foods
Wearing biodynamically and/or organically grown fibers, including those of hemp origins
Sharing seeds & agricultural knowledge freely & widely
Sharing our resources with each other
Moving from nonviolence to Peace
Saying a BIG **iFUCK YOU!** to Money (paper & coin currencies) & Credit (debt for the majority of people) whether issued by privately owned Central Bank systems and/or their governments (hence the "corporament"] as money & credit are Not Real & can Not Be eaTen!! ☺
Free Software & Hardware (ecologically designed) 4 ALL
Free ourselves from wage enslavement
Cultivate free love, imagination, creativity, peace, Truth, energy, electricity, bodies
Abolish state sanctioned Terrorism (death penalty, torture, experimentation, War, police & military apparatus {brutality}, ecological & thus human destruction, etc.]
Understand that THEY are here & have been for possibly thousands or millions of years
   Are we descendants of THEM?
How many presidents, prime ministers & other government leaders in the world share the same ancestry, i.e. the same or similar bloodlines?

Untitled: Controlled thoughts of ...

        Why?

                      Is this possible evidence of a global conspiracy?
      Who are they conspiring against?
      Who are the puppeteers?
      Who are the puppets?
What's Real(?]
      What's Fake?
Who created the Economy?

When was the last time that U played in the Earth, our Mother? Is it Global Warming, Global Cooling, Global Climate Change, or a Hoax played by the Elites (those who believe they have the power over all of US}?
Can Russia, the USA, and/or celestial beings {not from the Earth originally] alter the climate & weather on this planet?
      Have they manipulated our minds/bodies/spirits, clouds, precipitation, storms, land masses, water, food supply, flora & fauna on our Mother Earth?
      Why?
      Global domination perhaps?
            Galactic dominion?
      A quick means to depopulation & forcing people to become mentally/spiritually/emotionally/physically enslaved on a massive scale?

EduKate Urself & others.
Read the Labels --

                            of candidates
                            ofmedicines

Untitled: Controlled thoughts of ...

                    of foods
                    of cleaning products
                    of clothing
                    of transportation
options
                    of electrical products
                    of energy sources
                    of media pundits
                    of teachers
                    of leaders
                    of Religions (including
the Sciences)
                    of those around U

Relearn to see & feel Ur own energies & those of others
Become reacquainted with Ur lost tongue (other spoken & non-spoken languages -- i.e. verbal & nonverbal communication techniques

Realize that communism, socialism, and capitalism were created & are maintained by the global elites with THEIR currencies & THEIR credit
Create & invest in REAL community wealth

Rain gardens
Local farms
Urban gardens
Community gardens
Gardens on golf courses
Abandoned lot gardens
Home-basedgardens

Untitled: Controlled thoughts of ...

Composting
Vermiculture
Freeganism
Gifting Economy
Gift Economy
Cooperatives
Roof gardens
Forests
Prairie Lands
Green Belt Movements
Water the roots
Remember the micronutrients
¡¡Soil is aLive!!
Native vegetation & fauna
Seed collectives/banks
Share
School gardens
Institution gardens
Fair Trade & Living/Family Wages
Biodiversity
Smile
Share wisdom
Hug trees
Act Real
Plant organic & biodynamic goodness for now & the future

Let us remember that a puzzle is made up of different interlocking pieces

Synthetic biology is genetic engineering/biotechnology on

Untitled: Controlled thoughts of ...

<u>crack</u>ed up <u>speed</u>

Speak up B 4 U Lose your voice

What will U do today to save yourself (& thus the world?]

Cultivate a neu U

I hope that these assumedly (in Ur perceptive capabilities) random generated thoughts inspire U to action {pick up a rock, plant an organic/biodynamic seed, buy local food, start a seed bank, go outside & Play, read a book, go online & do authentic research, install Free Software and Hardware, write poetry, play music, find out who you are, Read the Labels, stand up for your cause, create an alternative, and so on} so that we can continue the creation of our World That Works for ALl of us [thank you Sharif Abdullah for your awe-inspiring books & informative website)

Are we reincarnations of each other?
Are we descendants of alien species?

Where do we go from here?
Financial meltdown thus more enslavement or to True Freedom?
                       Who will decide?
                       Is your retirement safe?
                       Is your nation's economy safe?
                       Is your unlabeled food or drink safe
to eat or drink?
                       They wouldn't poison powdered milk,

Untitled: Controlled thoughts of...

would THEY?

How do we separate Truth from Fiction, half-Truths from disinformation from outright lies from misinformation from distortions from faulty intelligence?

How do we move beyond Recycling?
How do we become good rather than **less** bad?

How {& when] should we imitate Nature & Natural processes & systems?
Why are any of these ideas important?
                    Or are they?
            Who decides?

If no one voted in an election, would THEY still pick the same puppet??
The legal definition of conspiracy is simply 2 or more individuals coming together to commit a criminal act. It **does not** require a whole government. A conspiracy is akin to a racket in which only a few insiders at the top of the pyramid know exactly what is going on (check out *War is a Racket* by Brigadier General Smedley Darlington Butler to better understand the nature of the war racket} & the others, if any, are only playing their role in whatever they have been told that they are participating in. This assumes that their mind has not been mind-controlled as then no explanation is needed to provide them with an impetus to act. Although I could be wrong. Thus, do the Research.
Seek out many sources of information.

Are they enlightened due to illuminating bodies?

##

Are we human-beings Intra- or Extra-Terrestrials? i.e. Are we birth or step-children of our Mother Earth?

Or are we just cosmic sparks of potentially entropic fields of electromagnetism surrounding superstrings of harmonic, kinetic rhythms displayed as genetic "human" markers?

Are some so-called "human" beings, in particular fields of professional endeavors, more of a continued & recent Extra-Terrestrial lineal origin than other human beings?

What does it mean to be a human being in this age?

Is there a global or galactic or universal Conspiracy in our midst?

Is the dog wagging his/her tail or is someone wagging the dog? [Check out the movie – *Wag the Dog*}

If there is some Conspiracy, then how do we (re)gain our individual & collective freedoms?

How do we open up our psychic & intuitive channels through our Third Eye therefore seeing through the fog blinding our 2 plain eyes?

Untitled: Controlled thoughts of...

How do we not only WAKE UP, but also GET UP?!

Fuck tha fog-makers
Fuck da "news"-fakers
Fuck dem wannabe Global Rulers
Fuck those that attempt to Enslave our Mental Wares
[Remember that Bob Marley sang that only WE can emancipate OURselves from mental slavery}

###

Fuck tha Intelligentsia from whence eYe sprang
Fuck the torturers & mercenaries
Fuck the uncaring
Fuck tha puppets & their puppeteers
Fuck tha "education"-fakers
Fuck da "corporament"
Fuck enslavement of all types [technological, wage/economic, chattel, physical, scientific & religious dogma, mental/emotional/spiritual/physiological/physical, sexual, school, prison, etc.}
Fuck limited ideas of profanity and/or obscenity
 Is poverty obscene?
 Is homelessness profane?
 Is dying from hunger or thirst in a world of excess food and water obscene and profane?
 Is choosing war and destruction over peace & love profane?
 Is corporate welfare obscene in its own right? [let alone discussing the humility & bureaucratic red-

tape along with the indignation people must endure to obtain pennies of human welfare while the corporations, as "citizens," receive billions, as a whole, annually w/ little to no fan-fare.)
Fuck pollution of all kinds
Fuck detention centers & interment camps [Who will they pick up 1st?}
Fuck tha militarized police and the counterparts in tha military (da "People Behind the Uniforms" MUST stand up & be counted!! ☺ }
Fuck tha Reptilian Agenda
Fuck the illusions of Economics (Money, Credit, Debt, Free Market Economics, Free Trade, Corporate Globalization, Corporate Welfare, privately-owned Central Bank(ers) posing as Government institutions]
Fuck tha enslavers
Fuck doze entities that abuse young beings, humans in particular, to bring fruition their Reptilian Agenda
Fuck Big Pharma
Fuck Flat-Earth Medicine
Fuck freedom-haters
Fuck GE, GMOs, Biotechnological Bullshit, Eugenics, Synthetic Biology
Fuck those that lead the sheep, oops -- people (men & womyn) astray intentionally & w/o remorse
Fuck tha Dis-ease Creators {Cancers too)
Fuck those that withhold [crucial) knowledge from all of US
Fuck is a powerful, emotive word
Fuck others I have missed & have not included on this brief list of Fuck-Yous as opposed to traditional Shout-outs

Untitled: Controlled thoughts of ...

What tha Fuck was I thinkin' writin' this Shit to fracture our incomplete worldview of "how the world really works?"

I actually hoped that you had the answers to that somewhat rhetorical ?.

Anything else to say here?

Jus' do Ur own research <u>as usual</u> and reach your own conclusions.

Remember that we can not change what we do not acknowledge and what we fear.
We must embrace LOVE & not fear in this great time of Uncertainty. The private-banking "money" creative lenders only have temporary power, i.e. until we dethrone them & create our own community-based economic systems & currencies based on REAL wealth, justice, fairness, equity, transparency, ecological competency (environmental, economic, social), equality, freedom & responsibility, and a new <u>vision</u> of U & Me!

[Yes, that was yet anotha' list!!)

Please feel free to let me know what U think of tha ideas continued in these lines of thought.
Let's build the World that is POSSIBLE!!!

B4 I 4GET: Let me send OUT a **BIG** Fuck U to tha population controllers & their sterilizers

Untitled: Controlled thoughts of ...

####

Fuck Bullshit Fake Material/Spiritual Science
Fuck pollution in all forms, spheres, and realms
Fuck Nanotechnology
Fuck tha enslaving attributes of High Technology
Fuck Flat-Earth Feeling, Thinkin', Seein', Believing, and Being
Fuck Flat-Earth Science

Any more ~~shout-outs~~ Fuck-U outs?

Yea, 1 more
          Fuck INDEPENDENCE!!!
I support, oops -- I mean WE, support
                        Interdependence as all
of us are at once One in a Universal fabric of interwoven webs
while alluding to distinct strands in Life

We all ~~breathe Air~~ swim in Air
We all sprang from the union of Mother Earth/Father Sky
We all are moved by the Moon & experience the Sun
We all exist as vibrations beating different chords (*)

* We are therefore all forms of potentially Kinetic Energies

We all experience a Consciousness
We are all present for a purpose and reason at this particular intersection of the Universe
We are all temporary and transient
We are all uniquely similar

Untitled: Controlled thoughts of ...

We are the puzzle pieces that make up the picture of our won worlds in the Universal Reality
We are all Created and thus Divinely Creative
We are all images and illusions based on frequencies
We are all data stored as binary bit types of code in a hexadecimal storage device decoding intricacies of parabolic substance in an over-reaching supportive glue of undue proverbial winds tonaling ringtones in this closed, yet open boundary system imitating our Actuality on tha other side resembling more of the Truth than we can decipher wit our limited, falsely understanding of our tools
We are all needed and wanted <u>now</u>
We are always where we are -- everywhere, somewhere, and nowhere -- at once
We all observe and are observed
We all entertain H_2O
We all manifest
We all know
We are all alive (though asleep in Reality and Awake over there in the True Ultimate Reality}
We all live out a particular purpose
What do we know?
We all know
We are all differently similar
We are all expressions in an algebraic expression fuddled with varying degrees of variables
Unity does not mean the same -- a puzzle is one story of different pieces
Ya dig?!

Separate & connected

#####

I haven't written out anything in a creative, poetically charming manner in a long ... time

Creating a Neu Model of Health & Wellness
= creating a New Vision of U & I
= creating a New Way of Gathering, Growing, Catching, and Exploring oUr Relationships with the Web of Life and thus the Foods that we ingest
= moving from an Ecological View of Health & Medicine → Universal View of Health & Medicine
= Loving More
= Balance
= Quality
= Breathing (Spirit)
= Evolving in a dynamically interlinked & interdependent Universal order
= Embracing the Past, Present, and tha Future
= Wholeness rather than Separation -- the Ultimate Illusion
= Knowing the Self's self
= Recognizing the wave/particle duality of all Life thus adding complexity to the murky waters of hypocrisy
= Resurrecting the Divine Creative Spark within the Whole Totality of Us
= Being "Reading the Labels" Literate
= Focusing on Cooperation > Competition

Untitled: Controlled thoughts of ...

= Seaing the Invisible (to tha Naked Is) Fields of Spiritual Influence along with the visible Spirits in AIL of Us
= Exploring the vast Possibilities of the Multi-Dimensional Universes
= Truth > Lies ☺
= Freedom and Openness through Sharing and Transparency
= Asking ?s and asking more ?s and ... asking even more ?s to elucidate more ?s and answers
= Making each of us healing patients
= Healing rather than Treating
= Forgiveness
= No Más mechanical, interchangeable machinery Philosophies
= a True Revolution
= Whole, Spherical, Multi-Dimensional Earth Thinkin'
= Challenging the status quo
= Envisioning a New World, a New Way, a Neu U and I (Us]
= Creating a Wholistic, Dynamic, Evolving, Vision of Health & Wellness and thus a Healthy State while creating a similar view of "dis-ease" and thus a "dis-eased state"
= Victimhood → Survivorhood
= Understanding the Whole Conception of Ever-Evolving Life Processes in a networked, systemic Web of Life (including our Purposes on the micro and macro levels}
= Integrative, Complementary Alternative Choices
= Our <u>very</u> words <u>and</u> Intentions have a vibrational energy
= Energies Can and Do Resonate with other Energies in a Fluidous, Complex, Dynamic, Orbiting, Elliptical, Spherical Reality
= Laughter and Humility
= Seek through the Inner → Outer

Untitled: Controlled thoughts of ...

= Correcting Our Mistakes
= How do U feel on each Level of Ur Existence?
= End the Warfare through Drugging (various biochemical stimuli above and beyond over-the-counter/prescription drugs included here), Antibiotics/Antibacterials, Radiation, Genetic Manipulative Alterations, and Immunizations/Vaccinations
= Who are We?
= God/Goddess are Loving!! ☺
= Possession is an Illusions
= Release the tension
= Body (Spiritual/Mental, Physical, and Emotional Layers/Levels) and not a Mind/Body/Spirit Split
= We are our Environment
= Bathe in Sunlight = Colored Vibrational Frequencies
= Each 1 Teach 1 in all stages of a developing Life
= Imagination
= No más Elitism
= Movement through the Dimensions
= Musical Vibrational Energy Frequencies of Varied Tonalities
= the Choices are Up to US
= Where do ~~we~~ WE go from Here?

######

Biochemical?
                    I thought that we were through with the illusory medical terminology, well -- are we?
~~Biochemical~~ Vibrational wave packets of encoded information forming fluid geometric patterns enabling biochmicogephysical markers for identification by a mechanistic, material, flat-earth,

physical scientific dogma (is a better statement of intended energy, i.e. information]

#######

Treating?
              What?
Treating the body's symptoms through suppressive technologies thereby malignantly directing the immunonetworks' decisions & causing other symptoms to appear on other levels as signs of disrupted energy flows, i.e. the allopathic view of the symptoms as the "dis-ease" and their choice to treat the "dis-ease" rather than help the person heal

Universal View of Health & Medicine?
1st - Our health is impacted directly and/or indirectly from the farthest realms of the Universes and the various dimensions within those Bodies
2nd - The Milky Way Galaxy
3rd - The solar system
4th - The Earth, Our Mother, and <u>her</u> levels of Existence & the Sky, Our Father, and <u>his</u> levels of Existence
5th - Our race of beings (the collective human consciousness)
6th - The nation
7th - The society
8th - The local bioregion
9th - The local ecosystem
10th - The family
11th - The multidimensional "individual" being

Consult *The Science of Homeopathy* by George Vithoulkas, *Vibrational Medicine: The #1 Handbook of Subtle-Energy Therapies* by Richard Gerber, M.D., and other sources for a more thorough discussion of these phenomena

We can not limit our understanding of health & wellness
We must extend it to the farthest reaches of the Ultimate Reality

Keep the ?'s coming ...

########

Is allopathic (modern "scientific" medicine) akin to torture?
∴ (Mathematical symbol for <u>therefore</u>), are we individuals that use that system of medicine freely, of our own will, committing self-torture?
Why would we knowingly and/or unknowingly condemn ourselves & our loved ones?
Don't we know that plenty of alternative and/or complementary options exist?
Or has that door been concealed to most of us?
Or is it that we would prefer a microwave symptomatic recovery rather than an extended time to properly complete the curative process from the inside → outside?

Do we care more about physical appearances (clothing, hairstyles, etc. of an aesthetic nature) of ourselves & others over our very own health and the health of our race?
Why do we make the easy choices now thus resulting in costlier

Untitled: Controlled thoughts of...

($ & health = freedom) decisions later?

Does your physician know more about U & Ur health than you do? Isn't it time that <u>YOU</u> become more responsible for your health?

Isn't it past time that we clean-up our collective messes to improve the health of our race & the rest of the Earthly inhabitants, including Mother Earth/Father Sky?

Why do we still thirst for War & bloodshed in the 21st Century of the Gregorian solar calendar? Why haven't we evolved beyond this desire? Have we been e-volving or de-volving? When will we, collectively & individually, change? Do we need more horrifically debilitating "dis-eases" to embrace our race's beings to guide us in new (or old useful tracks of positive evolution) paths?
Do we **really** care about each other?
Aren't we all interconnected & interrelated in a Universal Web of Life?

Why choose "dis-ease" = disorder = enslavement to the Medical Mafia and the drug overlords with their suppressive toxic chemical agents > health = freedom = happiness = peace = order?

#########

Is it that we do not know the true Nature of "dis-ease" progression nor that of health?

Or is it that we have closed-off our subtle sensitivities in this overly matterialistic (matter + materialistic) False Reality Show that we interpret as Truth?

Has human "progress" <u>dead</u>ened our forgotten, but not extinct, Senses?

Have we forgotten the Sacred Patterns of Our inner & outer Universes?

Is there a historically, collective Conspiracy to attempt to Cloud our True Past, Present, and Potential Futures? Is "modern scientific medicine" only just one of the tools in this arsenal?

How long do we keep on our "individual" and collective shackles?

Does your ill health positively impact the Gross Domestic Product (GDP) of your country? ∴ Why would your nation choose to offer healing therapies rather than treatment (symptom suppression-based) therapies?

Do we still *hear* the subtle sounds of silence? Of the wind? Of the Earth? Of Fire? Of water? Of Spiritual Connections? Of our Soul emanating through our Spirit? Of the Universes? Of Creation? Of our Ancestors? Of our disorder = "dis-ease"? Of our health?

##########

Do U care more about Ur illusional outer appearance > Ur health?

Untitled: Controlled thoughts of ...

Do U care more about "modern conveniences" > Ur health?
Do U care more about bullshit-fucking "comfort" (if "dis-ease" is comforting) junk "food" (is it really food?) > Ur health?

REMEMBER, it's Ur health, i.e., not anyone else's -- thus it's Ur right **and** responsibility!

How many more beings must die due to their interactions w/ the Medical Mafia B 4 we ask WHY?

Does freedom exist when there is no health freedom?

Is radiation impacting Ur health?

Are sunspots & other solar activity increasing or decreasing? What does that mean for all of US?

How do the farthest reaches of the Universes & the other dimensions impact all of US?

Are U a willing and/or unwilling active and/or inactive participant and/or spectator in Ur own "dis-ease" progression?

What are you going to do?

Do U care? If U don't care, why not?

Do U "stay the course" or change it?

Untitled: Controlled thoughts of ...

Do U control Urself? Or do(es) (an)other entity(ies) control U?

Do U seek treatment or cure? Do U know the difference?

Is life expectancy and quality of life increasing or decreasing?

Do U choose to live happy & healthy or "dis-eased" & fucked-up (pain, misery, etc.)?

How do U respond to negative & positive stimuli?

Are we still being sterilized? (This time through genetically modified organisms {gmos} as the latter phase of global eugenics.)

Are U an addict? Are U lying to Urself? Do U want to remain an addict? What are U going to do?

Do U know how to breathe properly?

Are U more afraid of Life or Death?

Are you "living to die" or "dying to live?" Or are you "living to live?"

What do you do 4 relaxation & enjoyment?

Do you know how to relax & enjoy Life?

Do we get it?

Untitled: Controlled thoughts of ...

Do something GOOD 4 UrSelf!!

Do U drink water DAILY in adequate amounts? Do you know when you are acutely and/or chronically dehydrated? Do you get salts (more than sodium) in adequate amounts DAILY?

Answer the ?s 4 yourself & be truly honest to yourself!!

Credit/Debt = BULLSHIT!

Basically, I've said all of this to WAKE YOU The FUCK UP!

BE Kind to Urself!

Love Thyself!

Thank-Urself!

Why all the fucking ?'s{?}

To shock U & have U question REALity & do something about it

###########

Some Mo'

Plant indigenous or native perennial goodness in organics, biodynamics, permaculture, and other methods

To till or not to till

Untitled: Controlled thoughts of ...

Wild is good

Is it sun spots flaring or Global Warming?

How far in the farthest reaches of the multidimensional Universes can we detect in our Mother Earth/Father Sky's changes and the changes in ourselves?

How shallow or deep is our Reality?

Are U following me?

Ask more ?s and you'll seek more answers.

We are intimately Divine and thus we must FORGIVE. Heal your past lives.

Love and Peace Freely.

~~27 August 2008~~ 23 September 2008
2 January 2009
25 March 2009
4 July 2009
31 January 2010
11 March 2010
####### 18 March 2010, 17 July 2010
######## 17 July 2010
######### 29 August 2010

Untitled: Controlled thoughts of...

########## 12 July 2011
########### 24 September 2011

Untitled: The Sunset in Her Eyes

Do U remember when I would call U on my way to work & express to U these sentiments: "I just saw the sunset & I thought of --- U!"?

I saw the sunset again today and I remembered the beautiful light that radiates from your Spirit.
I also remembered our happiness when we shared that occasion over the phone.

On 2nd thought, was I remarking about the sunrise? I don't remember, but the feelings of peace, happiness, and serene love are still the same.

You and I possess tremendous amounts of light that we have shared with each other over the years. This is our greatest Spiritual connection.

The beautiful sky colors always remind me of your gorgeous Smile & your laughing and playful Self.

I look forward to both the Sunset & the Sunrise as I look forward to sharing the beauty in the world with U.

I love You --- My Love!! ☺

13 December 2008

Myths in 2009 and Hopes for the Future

The year of 2009 in the Gregorian Calendar System is rapidly coming to a close and we are holding steadfastly to many myths and are still believing many lies. The following is a list of 4 of the lies maintained throughout this year:

1) **Myth**: Jesus Christ of Nazareth was born to his mother, the Virgin Mary, on December 25.

Reality: December 25 is not the actual birth date of Jesus Christ as his actual birth date was not written in *The Holy Bible*. But, there was a celebration during this time of year: *Dies Natalis Solis Invicti*, in Latin, which translates to "the birthday of the unconquered Sun" in English and this Celebration coincided with the Winter Solstice.
[Source: Wikipedia article on Christmas (https://en.wikipedia.org/wiki/Christmas)]

Furthermore, Jesus Christ did not die on the cross, which the Roman Empire used for Capital Punishment, but rather he died with his wife, Mary Magdalene, whom he had 3 children with, many years later in France.
[Sources: The following three books by Sylvia Browne: *If You Could See What I See: The Tenets of Novus Spiritus*, *Secrets & Mysteries of the World*, and *Secret Societies...and How They Affect Our Lives Today*. And KRS-One's "The Truth" off of his self-titled album (http://lyrics.wikia.com/KRS-One:The_Truth)]

2) **Myth**: War is fought by troops on behalf of their fellow citizens.

Reality: "WAR is a racket. It always has been. It is possibly the oldest, easily the most profitable, surely the most vicious. It is the only one international in scope. It is the only one in which the profits are reckoned in dollars and the losses in lives. A racket is best described, I believe, as something that is not what it seems to the majority of the people. Only a small 'inside' group knows what it is about. It is conducted for the benefit of the very few, at the expense of the very many. Out of war a few people make huge fortunes."
[Source: *War is a Racket* by Bridagier General Smedley D. Butler and Wikipeia article on War Is a Racket (https://en.wikipedia.org/wiki/War_is_a_Racket)]

"I helped make Mexico, especially Tampico, safe for American oil interests in 1914. I helped make Haiti and Cuba a decent place for the National City Bank boys to collect revenues in. I helped in the raping of half a dozen Central American republics for the benefits of Wall Street. The record of racketeering is long. I helped purify Nicaragua for the international banking house of Brown Brothers in 1909-1912. I brought light to the Dominican Republic for American sugar interests in 1916. In China I helped to see to it that Standard Oil went its way unmolested."
[Source: Speech made by Bridagier General Smedley D. Butler, http://www.fas.org/man/smedley.htm]

Wars going back to antiquity have been based on deception and all Wars have always been Civil Wars as we are all brothers and sisters. The continued US Wars of Aggression against the peoples of Iraq, Afghanistan, and people worldwide are based on lies. The events of 11 September 2001 did not bring about the War of Aggression against the people of Afghanistan. It was planned before that day and also the controlled demolition of the World Trade Center Towers 1, 2, and 7, were caused by high-tech weapons (scalar/plasma weapons) and/or the use of controlled demolitions (thermite). There were not 4 hijacked planes and the Pentagon was not hit by an airplane on its side that was under renovation then. There has not been a truly thorough investigation into those crimes. The US did not embark on a full-scale War of Aggression against the people of Iraq because of the alleged excuse of Weapons of Mass Destruction. It was to force the Iraqi government to use the US petrodollar rather than the European euro for petroleum transactions and to create a market for genetically modified "foods" (GMOs) in Iraq amongst other things. (The US/UK had continued to illegally bomb Iraq in the illegitimate "no-fly zones" for many years after the cease-fire agreement ended the "Persian Gulf War".)
[Sources: http://www.questionuniverse.com/rethink.html, http://questionuniverse.com/oldway/realitieswar.html, http://questionuniverse.com/oldway/iraqpage.html, and http://questionuniverse.com/oldway/continuum.html]

3) **Myth**: Climate Change is not real.

Reality: Climate Change is real and happens at the micro- and at the macro-levels in our Mother Earth/Father Sky daily and has since the beginning of time. Climate Change occurs due to the Earth's biological/geological/chemical processes and also the activities of human beings. The activities of humans include, but are not limited to, the following: cloud seeding, the spreading of Chemtrails, and the deliberate environmental modification of our Climate by military operations domestically and globally.

4) **Myth**: There has been a "health care" debate in the US.

Reality: There is no true discussion of health care and what it really means. There has been little discussion about prevention or about what it means to be healthy. There are numerous questions that have yet to be probed fully:

How many people die a year, globally, due to their interactions with the main Western system of "medicine" – allopathic medicine?
Why do we have health insurance companies?
Why did they come into existence?
What did people do before they existed?
Can we create alternatives to the current "health care" system?
Can we have the freedom to choose our own modes of healing?
What is "dis-ease?"
How can a person prevent a "dis-ease?"
What is true health – is it only the absence of "dis-ease"?
What is an ecological view of health and wellness?
Is the "germ theory of disease" accurate or is it a myth?
Why is the main Western system of "medicine" based on flat-

earth assumptions about the nature of healing and "dis-ease" in a spherical world?

Why does the main Western system of "medicine" treat the "dis-ease" (i.e. a person's symptoms brought about by the immune system) rather than promoting a person's natural curative abilities?

Why are human beings and the rest of the inhabitants of the Earth (including the living and breathing Mother Earth/Father Sky) treated as machines with expendable parts?

What are the levels of human existence and how do they affect our health?

How do food and other biochemical stimuli (including food additives) that we ingest through our skin (the largest organ), our nostrils, our eyes, our ears, and our mouths affect our health?

This brief discussion of the Myths and Realities of 2009 brings me to my hopes for 2010 and beyond.

I hope that human beings find inner peace by taking the time to know themselves and thus the Universes and realize that there is no Separation. Separation is an illusion. We are all strands in the Web of Life and what happens to one strand directly and/or indirectly impacts all strands. Furthermore, we must become (or continue) to be actively engaged in positive ecological (encompassing the social, economic, and environmental integrated spheres of existence) movements to resurrect our sense of purpose and connection with ourselves, our Mother Earth/Father Sky and all of her inhabitants. There are too many movements to name so just head outside and plant an authentic (beyond organic) garden for starters!

22 December 2009

Printed in *The Key Newsjournal* in January or February 2010. The above work has been modified from the original version.

[Author's Note: The author did not transfer his copyright over to the newspaper so he retains his rights.]

Say Goodbye to Poverty

*"Poverty is the worst kind of violence."**
-Mohandas Karamchand (Mahatma) Gandhi

It's the 21st Century in the Gregorian Calendar system
And we still have billions of people living in poverty worldwide
      Material poverty
           Lack of food to eat (although there is enough food produced to feed everyone)**
           Lack of clean water
           Lack of physical shelter
           Lack of economic income and its associated benefits
      Spiritual poverty
           Disconnection from our place in the Universes
           Disconnection from our place in Mother Earth/Father Sky
           Disconnection from each other, thereby feeling alienated in a crowd
           Disconnection from our very selves
And thus we continue in the worst form of violence

What can we DO?

We can create and support urban and rural (authentic) organic, biodynamic, ecological, naturally grown, sustainable gardens and farms that are GMO/GE-Free Zones to provide affordable, safe, and equitable access to culturally appropriate food worldwide

We can protect our waterways from pollution and end the "corporament" (corporate + government = "corporament") privatization of Water and with it the Water Wars

We can rehabilitate existing buildings to make them suitable for living

We can create our own local economies and currencies based on cooperation, "enoughness," and the well-being of all members of our communities

We can become the Creative Visionaries of the 21st Century that make the violence of poverty obsolete

What are **YOU** going to do?

*Source: Wikiquote page on Mohandas Karamchand Gandhi. http://en.wikiquote.org/wiki/Gandhi.

**Source: N. Sadik. Food and Agriculture Organization (FAO) of the United Nations Agriculture and Consumer Protection Department. "Population growth and the food crisis." http://www.fao.org/docrep/U3550t/u3550t02.htm.

14 March 2011

Ending Food Deserts

Let's end food deserts
        But, how?

Through
        Changing Zoning Ordinances
        Community Gardens
        Community Supported Agriculture (CSAs)
        Community Supported Seed & Food Banks
        Community Supported Kitchens
        Container Gardens
        Farmer's/Gardener's Markets
        Landscaping with Edible Plants
        Rooftop Gardens
        Sharing Our Bountiful Harvests
        Urban Farms & Gardens
        Yard Gardens

Let's provide food for ourselves, for all of the pollinators, and return our waste back to the Earth to create more food

\# 11 July 2011 (Published in *The Contributor* in July or August 2011)

Health for All of Us

wHole being
rEsponsibility for the choices that we make in every moment
Awareness in every moment
Love yourself enough to care
Influenced by our individual actions (six senses & what we put in and on our bodies) and how we reacT to both external and internal stimuli in our multidimensional selves to our Family to our Geographical Location to our Immediate Society to our Nation to our Earth to our Solar System to our Milky Way Galaxy to our Universe to the other known and unknown Universes & all of the dimensions or levels of existence present*
Happiness is our Divine Right

* I am grateful for *The Science of Homeopathy* by George Vithoulkas for my understanding of the influences on our Health above and beyond our individual selves

* I am grateful for *Vibrational Medicine: The #1 Handbook of Subtle-Energy Therapies* by Richard Gerber, M.D. for a thorough discussion of the various human dimensions

21 August 2011

Water for Life

Wa...wa...wa..ter is the life blood of Gaia, the Earth and is the center of our birth
Water, we are sorry for taking you, and thus us, for granted
We have soiled you with air, aquatic, and terrestrial pollution
We have forgotten that our very own health depends on good water quality
and not just the health of all other life on Gaia, the Earth
Water provides us with her good and her bad in a balancing effort
Let us remember that water vapor is a greater greenhouse gas than all of the other greenhouse gases combined
Let us remember that we need the infiltration of cleaner water into the groundwater system
Let us remember that water is a vibrational energy like all other Life (all matter) throughout the Universe
Let us remember that water remembers (has memory), that water is alive, and that we should be formless, like water, as Bruce Lee suggested
And lastly I end with I love you water and thank you water

20 April 2012

Afterword

How was the journey? Now that you've reached the end of this book I'll offer some parting thoughts.

Why have I decided to publish this personal book in this age of mega surveillance by the galactic/global elite? It's simple — this book is a vehicle for my personal healing and it may be useful for others in their healing journey too. In addition, the antidote to the surveillance is not for us to disconnect from each other and to live in isolated fear, but it is for us to reconect with each other, remember who we really are, and be FREE. (I am including other antidotes, in the form of resources, at the end of this section.)

Along with the massive surveillance, we are in an age of geoengineering (chemtrails, etc.), radiochemical releases, mind control/manipulation (including mis- and dis-information), and other forms of electromagnetic pollution. I ask that all beings working on these and other negatively destructive projects to reclaim your loving Soul and to cease working on those projects.

I recommend that we continue practicing healing forms of agriculture (biodynamic/homeopathic agriculture & the positive use of magnets, acoustic, and other vibrational energies), continue using vibrational energy healing systems, forgive ourselves and each other, and elevate our Collective Human Consciousness. One reason that we are going through these trials and tribulations, is that we have polluted our Collective

Afterword

Consciousness with fear and all of its negative descendants rather than empowering our Collective Consciousness with love and peace. Let us remember that we are the Universal Creator having an experience as human beings.

You will find the aforementioned topics, and many others, discussed in the books contained on the resource pages that follow. [Please note that the authors of the resources have not endorsed me nor my book & I do not endorse all of the ideas and conclusions found in the resources.]

Regarding the editing of this book, I tried to keep my original intent as much as possible while making revisions. With some of the pieces the formatting has been altered from the original typed document (8.5 in x 11 in) to what is contained in this book (4.7 in x 6.2 in).

I used the following Free/Libre and Open Source Software (FLOSS) fonts (yes, fonts are software):

on the front cover: StayPuft, Musica, Ecolier_court, FreeSans, Elegante, Linux Libertine Display O, and Liberation Sans;
on the back cover: Bitstream Vera Serif and Bitstream Vera Sans; and
on the spine: Dutismo, DejaVu Serif, Dynamic BRK, Fanwood, Free Schoolbook, and Linden Hill.
Most, if not all, of the aforementioned fonts can be found

Afterword

at the Open Font Library (http://www.openfontlibrary.org) and/or in your favorite, free GNU/Linux distribution.

I used both Inkscape (http://inkscape.org) and the GIMP (GNU Image Manipulation Program) [http://www.gimp.org] for the creation of the front and back covers & the spine.

For the storage and editing of this book, I started out using OpenOffice.org Writer (now Apache OpenOffice) [https://openoffice.apache.org], but I moved to LibreOffice Writer (http://www.libreoffice.org) over the past couple of years.

I used Tellico (http://tellico-project.org) and OpenOffice.org/LibreOffice Writer for the storage of the print resources.

For the final design & layout of the book, I used Scribus (http://www.scribus.net).

All of the recent work has been performed on the fully free GNU/Linux based operating system called Trisquel (http://trisquel.info).

Although I am a supporter of Free/Libre and Open Source Software (FLOSS) and Free/Libre Hardware, I recognize the downsides of our mainstream state of (high) technology and thus offer these resources:

What Biotechnology, Genetic Engineering, Synthetic Biology, Cloning, Nanotechnology, High-Technology (High Tech), Conventional Renewable Energy Technologies (Solar, Geothermal, Wind, etc.), and Related Technologies are missing (http://www.ecoccs.com/resources_links.html#missing)

Afterword

Negative Effects of High-Technology (High Tech)
[http://www.ecoccs.com/resources_links.html#hightech]

ElectroMagnetism and Adverse Health Effects
(http://www.ecoccs.com/resources_links.html#em_health)

Below are some resources that can serve as an antidote to the galactic/global surveillance complex:

Global Police State/Surveillance
(http://www.questionuniverse.com/rethink.html#surv)

Digital/Internet Freedom
(http://www.ecoccs.com/resources_links.html#dig_free)

Break Out of Surveillance
(http://www.ecoccs.com/resources_links.html#break_free)

Welcome to the Machine: Science, Surveillance, and the Culture of Control. Derrick Jensen and George Draffan. ISBN# 978-1-931498-52-4

Thank you for joining me on this journey! Take care. Peace be unto you. ☺

6, 8, 12, 14 – 15, and 18 February 2014

About the Author

Who am I? I am, like you and everyone else, the Universal Creator. Each one of us is having an "individual" experience in this illusionary Reality that causes us to believe that we are a separate being, rather than the loving Universal Creator.

I am called Irucka Ajani Embry, which is the name of the experiential vehicle that I am occupying in this lifetime. I am an evolving, perfectly imperfect being born into a supportive village of family and friends in Lexington, Kentucky.

Irucka is a life long teacher and student. He sees himself as a being, which Irucka feels connects him more fully to all beings and not solely to other human beings. He credits this idea of connection, rather than separation, to the family (especially his father) and friends that encompassed the village that helped to raise Irucka and his older siblings. It is that springboard that allowed him to question Reality and make seen and unseen connections at an early age. Irucka continues to employ those skills in his professional life as an environmental engineer-in-training and business owner & in his personal life through the various creative and imaginative pathways that he cultivates. His main creative outlet, other than writing and music, is gardening. Irucka recognizes that the most healthy food will be grown in healthy and lively soil that is wetted by healthy water.

About the Author

He shares these and many other ideas, learned through experience or from interactions with others, mostly through written expressions. Irucka has had his work printed in the following publications: Health & Wellness magazine, Lexington Herald-Leader (http://www.kentucky.com), The Key Newsjournal (http://keyconversationsradio.com), University of Tennessee's The Daily Beacon (http://utdailybeacon.com), Tennessee Independent Media Center (now defunct), English version of the Russian paper Pravda (http://english.pravda.ru), and The Contributor (http://thecontributor.org).

Irucka recognizes that he doesn't yet exemplify his highest ideas expressed in his creative expressions, but he will prior to leaving this plane of existence.

In order to release more of his thoughts unfiltered he created Questioning the Universe Publishing (QUP) [http://www.questionuniverse.com], which is a publisher of bookmarks, books, electronic books (e-books), Hip Hop music, and postcards.

January/February 2014

Appendix

Resourcical (R)Evolutionary Tacticals

Revolution

Expanding Horizons Through Creative Expressions: Reflections and Thoughts Related to the Struggle for Peace, Sustainability, Equality, and the Search for Humanity. Obiora Embry. ISBN# 978-0-9897507-0-7

The Next American Revolution: Sustainable Activism for the Twenty-First Century. Grace Lee Boggs with Scott Kurashige. ISBN# 0-520-27259-5

Living For Change: An Autobiography. Grace Lee Boggs. ISBN# 0-8166-2955-2

Conversations in Maine: Exploring Our Nation's Future. James and Grace Lee Boggs & Freddy and Lyman Paine. ISBN# 0-89608-008-0

Racism and the Class Struggle: Further Pages from a Black Worker's Notebook. James Boggs. ISBN# 0-85345-164-8

The American Revolution: Pages from a Negro Worker's Notebook. James Boggs. ISBN# 978-0-85345-015-3

Seven Seeds for a New Society. Sharif Abdullah. ISBN# 978-0-578-03252-8

Creating a World That Works for All. Sharif Abdullah. ISBN# 1-57675-062-0

The Power of One: Authentic Leadership in Turbulent Times. Sharif Abdullah. ISBN# 0-86571-325-1

Callus On My Soul: A Memoir. Dick Gregory with Shelia P. Moses. ISBN# 978-0-7582-0202-4

Nigger: An Autobiography. Dick Gregory with Robert Lipsyte. ISBN# 978-0-671-73560-9

Dick Gregory's Political Primer. Dick Gregory. ISBN# 978-0-06-080264-6

Seize the Time: The Story of the Black Panther Party and Huey P. Newton. Bobby Seale. ISBN# 978-0-933121-30-0

A Lonely Rage: The Autobiography of Bobby Seale. Bobby Seale. ISBN# 978-0-8129-0715-5

History

When the Earth Nearly Died: Compelling Evidence of a World Cataclysm 11,500 Years Ago. D. S. Allan and J. B. Delair. ISBN# 1-85860-008-1

Dead Men's Secrets: Tantalising Hints of a Lost Super Race. Jonathan Gray. ISBN# 978-1-57258-403-7

Disinformation Guide to Ancient Aliens, Lost Civilizations, Astonishing Archaeology & Hidden History. Edited by Preston Peet. ISBN# 978-1-938875-03-8

Technology of the Gods: The Incredible Sciences of the Ancients. David Hatcher Childress. ISBN# 978-0-932813-73-2

Ancient Inventions. Peter James and Nick Thorpe. ISBN# 978-0-345-40102-1

Ancient Mysteries. Peter James and Nick Thorpe. ISBN# 978-0-345-43488-3

Black Genesis: The Prehistoric Origins of Ancient Egypt. Robert Bauval and Thomas Brophy. ISBN# 978-1-59143-114-5

A New View of the World: Handbook to the Peters Projection World Map. Ward L. Kaiser. ISBN# 978-1-931057-05-9

Lies My Teacher Told Me: Everything Your American History Textbook Got Wrong. James W. Loewen. ISBN# 978-0-7432-9628-1

A People's History of the United States: 1492-Present. Howard Zinn. ISBN# 978-0-06-052837-9

Before the Mayflower: A History of Black America. Lerone Bennett, Jr. ISBN# 978-0-14-017822-7

They Came Before Columbus: The African Presence in Ancient

America. Ivan Van Sertima. ISBN# 978-0-8129-6817-0

Christopher Columbus and the Conquest of Paradise. Kirkpatrick Sale. ISBN# 978-1-84511-154-0

Rethinking Columbus: The Next 500 Years. Edited by Bill Bigelow and Bob Peterson. ISBN# 978-0-942961-20-1

Black Indians: A Hidden Heritage. William Loren Katz. ISBN# 978-1-44244-637-3

IndiVisible: African-Native American Lives in the Americas. Gabrielle Tayac. ISBN# 978-1-58834-271-3

Galactic/Global Conspiracy (helping us understand what really is going on)

Illuminati in the Music Industry. Mark Dice. ISBN# 978-0-9887268-1-9

The Psychological Covert War on Hip Hop. Professor Griff. ISBN# 0-9771242-0-7

The Covert War Against Rock: What You Don't Know About the Deaths of Jim Morrison, Tupac Shakur, Michael Hutchence, Brian Jones, Jimi Hendrix, Phil Ochs, Bob Marley, Peter Tosh, John Lennon, and The Notorious B.I.G. Alex Constantine. ISBN# 0-922915-61-X

Overthrow of the American Republic: The Writings of Sherman Skolnick. Sherman H. Skolnick. ISBN# 978-1-893302-22-8

Ahead of the Parade: A Who's Who of Treason and High Crimes: Exclusive Details of Fraud and Corruption of the Monopoly Press, the Banks, the Bench and the Bar, and the Secret Political Police. Sherman H. Skolnick. ISBN# 978-1-893302-32-7

Monumental Myths of the Modern Medical Mafia and Mainstream Media and the Multitude of Lying Liars That Manufactured Them. Ty Bollinger. ISBN# 978-0-9788065-7-6

Death in the Air: Globalism, Terrorism & Toxic Warfare. Dr. Leonard G. Horowitz. ISBN# 978-0-923550-30-1

The Trillion-Dollar Conspiracy: How the New World Order, Man-Made Diseases, and Zombie Banks Are Destroying America. Jim Marrs. ISBN# 978-0-06-197069-6

The Cosmic Conspiracy. Stan Deyo. ISBN# 978-0-9727688-7-0

Our Occulted History: Do the Global Elite Conceal Ancient Aliens? Jim Marrs. ISBN# 978-0-06-213032-7

Alien Agenda: Investigating the Extraterrestrial Presence Among Us. Jim Marrs. ISBN# 978-0-06-095536-6

The Element Encyclopedia of Secret Societies. John Michael Greer. ISBN# 978-1-43511-088-5

The Element Encyclopedia of Secret Signs and Symbols. Adele Nozedar. ISBN# 978-1-43511-087-8

The Perception Deception. David Icke. ISBN# 978-0-9559973-8-9

Remember Who You Are. David Icke. ISBN# 0-9559973-3-X

Human Race Get Off Your Knees: The Lion Sleeps No More. David Icke. ISBN# 978-0-9559973-1-0

Infinite Love Is the Only Truth: Everything Else Is Illusion. David Icke. ISBN# 978-0-9538810-6-2

...And the Truth Shall Set You Free. David Icke. ISBN# 0-9538810-5-9

The David Icke Guide to the Global Conspiracy (and How to End It). David Icke. ISBN# 978-0-9538810-8-6

The Robots' Rebellion: The Story of the Spiritual Renaissance. David Icke. ISBN# 978-1-85860-022-2

Free Energy (Zero Point Energy)

Energy Abundance Now: A Brief History of Man's Quest for Energy: A New Energy Reference Book with a Practical Guide of Working Devices You Can Build: CD-ROM Included. Brian H. Berrett. ISBN# 1-42761-798-8

Tapping the Zero Point Energy. Moray B. King. ISBN# 978-1-931882-00-2

The Energy Machine of T. Henry Moray. Moray B. King. ISBN# 1-931882-42-8

The Energy Machine of Joseph Newman. Joseph Newman. ISBN# 0-9613835-2-6

Basic Principles of Over Unity Electromagnetic Machines: A Scientific View Into the World of Free Energy From Electric Charges and Magnetic Fields. Jovan Marjanovic, M.Sc. ISBN# 978-86-88-88301-6

The Orgone Accumulator Handbook: Wilhelm Reich's Life-Energy Discoveries and Healing Tools for the 21st Century, with Construction Plans. James DeMeo, Ph.D. ISBN# 978-0-9802316-3-2

The Energy Evolution: Harnessing Free Energy From Nature. Viktor Schauberger. ISBN# 978-1-85860-061-1

The Tesla Papers. Nikola Tesla. Edited by David Hatcher Childress. ISBN# 0-932813-86-0

The Fantastic Inventions of Nikola Tesla. Nikola Tesla. Edited by David Hatcher Childress. ISBN# 0-932813-19-4

Occult Ether Physics: Tesla's "Ideal Flying Machine" and the

Conspiracy to Conceal It. William Lyne.

Science

Blinded by Science. Matthew Silverstone. ISBN# 978-0-9568656-0-1

In The Minds of Men: Darwin and the New World Order. Ian T. Taylor. ISBN# 978-1-882510-15-3

The Holographic Universe: The Revolutionary Theory of Reality. Michael Talbot. ISBN# 978-0-06-201410-8

The Holotropic Mind: The Three Levels of Human Consciousness and How They Shape Our Lives. Stanislav Grof, M.D. with Hal Zina Bennett. ISBN# 978-0-06-250659-7

Psychoenergetic Science: A Second Copernican-Scale Revolution. William A. Tiller, Ph.D. ISBN# 978-142433-8

Morphic Resonance: The Nature of Formative Causation. Rupert Sheldrake. ISBN# 978-1-59477-317-4

Living Rainbow H_2O. Mae-Wan Ho. ISBN# 978-981-439089-7

The Rainbow and the Worm: The Physics of Organisms. Mae-Wan Ho. ISBN# 978-981-283260-3

The Systems View of Life: A Unifying Vision. Fritjof Capra and Pier

Luigi Luisi. ISBN# 978-1-10701-136-6

The Hidden Connections: A Science for Sustainable Living. Fritjof Capra. ISBN# 978-0-385-49472-4

The Web of Life: A New Scientific Understanding of Living Systems. Fritjof Capra. ISBN# 978-0-385-47676-8

The Tao of Physics: An Exploration of the Parallels between Modern Physics and Eastern Mysticism. Fritjof Capra. ISBN# 978-1-59030-835-6

The Sacred Balance: Rediscovering Our Place in Nature. David Suzuki with Amanda McConnell & Adrienne Mason. ISBN# 978-1-55365-166-6

Wisdom of the Elders: Sacred Native Stories of Nature. David Suzuki and Peter Knudtson. ISBN# 978-0-553-37263-2

Biomimicry: Innovation Inspired by Nature. Janine M. Benyus. ISBN# 978-0-06-053322-9

The Upcycle: Beyond Sustainability—Designing for Abundance. William McDonough and Michael Braungart. ISBN# 978-0-86547-748-3

Cradle to Cradle: Remaking the Way We Make Things. William McDonough and Michael Braungart. ISBN# 978-0-86547-587-8

Agriculture

My Work Is That of Conservation: An Environmental Biography of George Washington Carver. Mark D. Hersey. ISBN# 978-0-8203-3870-5

Plant Souls Speak. Robert Shapiro. ISBN# 1-891824-74-0

The Secret Teachings of Plants: The Intelligence of the Heart in the Direct Perception of Nature. Stephen Harrod Buhner. ISBN# 978-1-59143-035-3

Teaming with Microbes: The Organic Gardener's Guide to the Soil Food Web. Jeff Lowenfels and Wayne Lewis. ISBN# 1-60469-113-1

The War on Bugs. Will Allen. ISBN# 1-933392-46-0

Attracting Native Pollinators: Protecting North America's Bees and Butterflies. Xerces Society staff members Eric Mader, Matthew Shepherd, Mace Vaughan, and Scott Black in collaboration with Gretchen LeBuhn. ISBN# 978-1-60342-695-4

The Good Food Revolution: Growing Healthy Food, People, and Communities. Will Allen with Charles Wilson. ISBN# 1-59240-760-9

All New Square Foot Gardening. Mel Bartholomew. ISBN# 1-59186-202-7

Food Not Lawns: How to Turn Your Yard into a Garden and Your Neighborhood into a Community. Heather Coburn Flores. ISBN# 978-1-933392-07-3

Paradise Lot: Two Plant Geeks, One-Tenth of an Acre, and the Making of an Edible Garden Oasis in the City. Eric Toensmeier with Contributions from Jonathan Bates. ISBN# 978-1-60358-399-2

The Wild Gardener: On Flowers and Foliage for the Natural Garden. Peter Loewer. ISBN# 978-1-62268-009-2

A Field Guide to Edible Wild Plants of Eastern and Central North America. Lee Allen Peterson. ISBN# 0-395-92622-X

A Field Guide to Medicinal Plants and Herbs: Of Eastern and Central North America. Steven Foster and James A. Duke. ISBN# 978-039598-8

The Fertile Earth: Nature's Energies in Agriculture, Soil Fertilisation and Forestry. Viktor Schauberger. ISBN# 978-1-85860-060-4

Farmers of Forty Centuries: Organic Farming in China, Korea, and Japan. F. H. King. ISBN# 0-486-43609-8

Sowing Seeds in the Desert: Natural Farming, Global Restoration, and Ultimate Food Security. Masanobu Fukuoka. Edited by Larry Korn. ISBN# 978-1-60358-522-4

Four-Season Harvest: Organic Vegetables from Your Home Garden All

Year Long. Eliot Coleman. ISBN# 978-1-890132-27-9

Eco-Farm, An Acres U.S.A. Primer: The definitive guide to managing farm and ranch soil fertility, crops, fertilizers, weeds and insects while avoiding dangerous chemicals. Charles Walters. ISBN# 978-0-911311-74-7

Creating a Forest Garden: Working with Nature to Grow Edible Crops. Martin Crawford. ISBN# 978-1-900322-62-1

Gaia's Garden: A Guide to Home-Scale Permaculture. Toby Hemenway. ISBN# 1-60358-029-8

Sepp Holzer's Permaculture: A Practical Guide to Small-Scale, Integrative Farming and Gardening. Sepp Holzer. Translated by Anna Sapsford-Francis. ISBN# 978-1-60358-370-1

Homeopathy for Plants: A practical guide for indoor, balcony and garden plants with tips on dosage, use and choice of potency. Christiane Maute. ISBN# 3-943309-21-5

Homeopathy for Farm and Garden: The Homeopathic Treatment of Plants. Vaikunthanath Das Kaviraj. ISBN# 978-3-941706-47-7

A Biodynamic Farm: For Growing Wholesome Food. Hugh Lovel. ISBN# 978-0-911311-45-7

A Biodynamic Manual: Practical Instructions for Farmers and Gardeners. Pierre Masson. Translated by Monique Blais. ISBN# 978-086315-8

Biodynamic Gardening for Health & Taste. Hilary Wright. ISBN# 1-84000-622-6

Stolen Harvest: The Hijacking of the Global Food Supply. Vandana Shiva. ISBN# 978-0-89608-607-4

Seeds of Destruction: The Hidden Agenda of Genetic Manipulation. F. William Engdahl. ISBN# 978-0-937147-22-1

Genetic Roulette: The Documented Health Risks of Genetically Engineered Foods. Jeffrey M. Smith. ISBN# 978-0-9729665-2-8

GMO Free: Exposing the Hazards of Biotechnology to Ensure the Integrity of Our Food Supply. Mae-Wan Ho, Ph.D. and Lim Li Ching. ISBN# 978-1-890612-37-5

Health & Wellness

Dick Gregory's Natural Diet for Folks Who Eat: Cookin' With Mother Nature. Dick Gregory. Edited by James R. McGraw. ISBN# 978-0-06-080315-5

Black Gene Lies: Slave Quarter Cures. Dr. Joel D. Wallach, BS, DVM, ND and Dr. Ma Lan, MD, MS, LAc with Dr. Jennifer Daniels, BA, MD, MBA. ISBN# 0-9748581-3-7

How to Raise a Healthy Child... in Spite of Your Doctor. Robert S. Mendelsohn, M.D. ISBN# 978-0-345-34276-8

Obtaining Optimum Health: A Practical Guide to Removing Obstacles to Cure. Roger Dyson, Rona Francis, and Jóna Ágústa Ragnheiðardóttir. ISBN# 978-1-874581-09-3

Reader's Digest Family Guide to Natural Medicine: How to Stay Healthy the Natural Way. ISBN# 0-89577-433-X

The Water Wizard: The Extraordinary Properties of Natural Water. Viktor Schauberger. ISBN# 978-1-85860-048-2

The Hidden Messages in Water. Masaru Emoto. Translated by David A. Thayne. ISBN# 0-7432-8980-3

Flowforms: The Rhythmic Power of Water. John Wilkes. ISBN# 978-0-86315-392-1

Energizing Water: Flowform Technology and the Power of Nature. Jochen Schwuchow, John Wilkes, and Iain Trousdell. ISBN# 978-1-85584-240-3

The Case against Fluoride: How Hazardous Waste Ended Up in Our Drinking Water and the Bad Science and Powerful Politics That Keep It There. Paul Connett, PhD, James Beck, MD, PhD, and H. S. Micklem, DPhil. ISBN# 978-1-60358-287-2

Vibrational Medicine: The #1 Handbook of Subtle-Energy Therapies. Richard Gerber, M.D. ISBN# 1-879181-58-4

Passport To Aromatherapy. J. D. Wallach, BS, DVM, ND and Ma

Lan, MD, MS, LAc with Alexandria Brighton & Dr. Judy Wright. ISBN# 0-9748581-2-9

Energy Medicine: Balancing Your Body's Energies for Optimal Health, Joy, and Vitality. Donna Eden with David Feinstein, Ph.D. ISBN# 1-58542-650-4

Bioenergetic Medicines East and West: Acupuncture and Homeopathy. Clark A. Manning and Louis J. Vanrenen. ISBN# 1-55643-017-5

Chinese Acupuncture and Moxibustion. Cheng Xinnong. ISBN# 978-7-11905994-5

Biological, Chemical, and Nuclear Warfare: Protecting Yourself and Your Loved Ones: The Power of Digital Medicine. Savely Yurkovsky, MD. ISBN# 978-0-9726346-0-1

Applying Bach Flower Therapy to the Healing Profession of Homeopathy: Psychology, Psychiatry, Psychosomatic Medicine. Dr. Cornelia Richardson-Boedler, N.M.D., H.M.D., M.A., BCFM, MFCC. ISBN# 978-81-31-90755-9

Lectures on Homeopathic Philosophy. James Tyler Kent. ISBN# 978-1-60386-263-9

Homeopathy: Beyond Flat Earth Medicine. Timothy R. Dooley, N.D., M.D. ISBN# 978-1-886893-01-6

Discovering Homeopathy: Your Introduction to the Science and Art of

Homeopathic Medicine. Dana Ullman. ISBN# 978-1-55643-1

The Science of Homeopathy. George Vithoulkas. ISBN# 0-8021-5120-5

A New Model for Health and Disease. George Vithoulkas. ISBN# 1-55643-087-6

Homeopathy for Musculoskeletal Healing. Asa Hershoff, N.D., D.C. ISBN# 1-55643-237-2

Chiropractic Technique: Principles and Procedures. Thomas F. Bergmann and David H. Peterson. ISBN# 978-0-323-04969-6

The Chiropractic Evolution: Health From the Inside Out. David R. Moore, D.C. ISBN# 978-1-46377-340-3

Elements 4 Optimal Health. Dr. Jermaine Ware. ISBN# 978-1495414909

Core Health: The Quantum Way to Inner Power. Dr. Ed Carlson and Dr. Livia Kohn. ISBN# 1-62141-707-7

One Mind: How Our Individual Mind Is Part of a Greater Consciousness and Why It Matters. Larry Dossey, M.D. ISBN# 978-1-40194-315-8

The Bond: How to Fix Your Falling-Down World. Lynne McTaggart. ISBN# 978-1-43915-795-4

200,000,000 Guinea Pigs: New Dangers in Everday Foods, Drugs, and Cosmetics. John Grant Fuller. ISBN# 978-0-399-11000-9

Work With Your Doctor To Diagnose and Cure 27 Ailments With Natural and Safe Methods. Dr. Michael D. Farley, NMD and Ty M. Bollinger. ISBN# 978-0-9788065-5-2

The 9 Steps to Keep the Doctor Away: Simple Actions to Shift Your Body and Mind to Optimum Health for Greater Longevity. Dr. Rashid A. Buttar. ISBN# 978-0-9794302-4-4

Male Practice: How Doctors Manipulate Women. Robert S. Mendelsohn, M.D. ISBN# 978-0-8092-5721-8

The Medical Mafia: How to Get Out of it Alive and Take Back Our Health and Wealth. Guylaine Lanctot, M.D. ISBN# 978-2-9807465-2-9

Confessions of a Medical Heretic. Robert S. Mendelsohn, M.D. ISBN# 978-0-8092-4131-6

Green Medicine: Challenging the Assumptions of Conventional Health Care. Larry Malerba, D.O. ISBN# 978-1-55643-902-5

Dead Doctors Don't Lie. Dr. Joel D. Wallach and Dr. Ma Lan. ISBN# 978-0-9748581-0-4

Cancer: Step Outside the Box. Ty Bollinger. ISBN# 978-0-9788065-0-7

Forbidden Medicine: Is Effective Non-toxic Cancer Treatment Being Suppressed? Ellen Brown. ISBN# 978-0-9795608-3-5

Rethinking Cancer: Non-Traditional Approaches to the Theories, Treatments and Preventions of Cancer. Ruth Sackman. ISBN# 978-0-7570-0093-5

Healing the Gerson Way: Defeating Cancer and Other Chronic Diseases. Charlotte Gerson with Beata Bishop. ISBN# 978-0-9760186-2-9

Cancer is a Fungus: A Revolution in Tumor Therapy. Dr. T. Simoncini. ISBN# 88-87-24108-2

Bechamp or Pasteur?: A Lost Chapter in the History of Biology. Ethel D. Hume. ISBN# 978-0-9802976-0-7

Mirage of Health: Utopias, Progress, and Biological Change. René Dubos. ISBN# 978-0-8135-1260-0

When Antibiotics Fail: Restoring the Ecology of the Body. Marc Lappé. ISBN# 978-1-55643-191-3

Good-Bye Germ Theory: Ending a Century of Medical Fraud and How to Protect Your Family. Dr. William P. Trebing. ISBN# 1-41345-440-2

Vaccine Damaged Children: Treatment, Prevention, Reasons. Dr. Isaac Golden. ISBN# 0-9578726-6-6

Vaccine Free: Prevention and Treatment of Infectious Contagious Disease with Homeopathy. Kate Birch, RSHom(NA), CCH, CMT. ISBN# 978-1-48278-960-7

The Virus and the Vaccine: Contaminated Vaccine, Deadly Cancers, and Government Neglect. Debbie Bookchin and Jim Schumacher. ISBN# 978-0-312-34272-2

AIDS Inc.: Scandal of the Century. Jon Rappoport. ISBN# 978-0-941523-03-5

Emerging Viruses: AIDS and Ebola: Nature, Accident, or Intentional? Leonard G. Horowitz, D.M.D., M.A., M.P.H. ISBN# 978-0-923550-12-7

State Origin: The Evidence of the Laboratory Birth of AIDS. Boyd Ed Graves. ISBN# 0-9707735-1-X

Economics

Money Creators. Gertrude M. Coogan. ISBN# 0-317-53299-5

Billions for the Bankers: Debts for the People. Sheldon Emry.

The Secrets of the Federal Reserve. Eustace Mullins. ISBN# 978-0-9799176-5-3

The Creature from Jekyll Island: A Second Look at the Federal Reserve.

G. Edward Griffin. ISBN# 978-0-912986-45-6

The Federal Reserve Conspiracy. Antony C. Sutton. ISBN# 978-0-944379-08-0

The Global Economic Crisis: The Great Depression of the XXI Century. Edited by Michel Chossudovsky and Andrew J. Marshall. ISBN# 0-9737147-3-5

Web of Debt: The Shocking Truth About Our Money System and How We Can Break Free. Ellen Hodgson Brown, J.D. ISBN# 978-0-9833308-5-1

The Public Bank Solution: From Austerity to Prosperity. Ellen Brown. ISBN# 978-0-9833308-6-8

Rethinking Money: How New Currencies Turn Scarcity into Prosperity. Bernard Lietaer and Jacqui Dunne. ISBN# 978-1-60994-296-0

What Comes After Money?: Essays from Reality Sandwich on Transforming Currency and Community. Edited by Daniel Pinchbeck and Ken Jordan. ISBN# 978-1-58394-349-6

Hometown Money: How to Enrich Your Community with Local Currency. Paul Glover. ISBN# 978-0-9622911-3-5

Capitalism: A Ghost Story. Arundhati Roy. ISBN# 978-1-60846-385-5

11 September 2001 and the "War on Terrorism"

Where Did the Towers Go?: Evidence of Directed Free-energy Technology on 9/11. Judy Wood, B.S., M.S., Ph.D. ISBN# 978-0-615-41256-6

America's "War on Terrorism". Michel Chossudovsky. ISBN# 978-0-9737147-1-5

9/11 Synthetic Terror: Made in USA. Webster Griffin Tarpley. ISBN# 0-930852-37-0

The Terror Conspiracy Revisited: What Really Happened on 9/11 and Why We're Still Paying the Price. Jim Marrs. ISBN# 978-1-934708-63-7

Alice in Wonderland and the World Trade Center Disaster: Why the Official Story of 9/11 is a Monumental Lie. David Icke. ISBN# 978-0-9538810-2-4

War

Water Wars: Privatization, Pollution, and Profit. Vandana Shiva. ISBN# 978-0-89608-650-0

Towards a World War III Scenario: The Dangers of Nuclear War. Michel Chossudovsky. ISBN# 978-0-9737147-5-3

War Is a Racket: The Anti-War Classic by America's Most Decorated General, Two Other Anti-Interventionist Tracts, and Photographs from the Horror of It. Major General Smedley D. Butler. ISBN# 0-922915-86-5

Maverick Marine: General Smedley D. Butler and the Contradictions of American Military History. Hans Schmidt. ISBN# 0-8131-0957-4

The War Racket: The Lies, Myths, and Propaganda That Feed the American War Machine. Harry Browne. ISBN# 978-0-7852-6249-7

The Protection Racket State: Elite Politics, Military Extortion, and Civil War in El Salvador. William Stanley. ISBN# 978-1-56639-392-8

Hideous Dream: A Soldier's Memoir of the US Invasion of Haiti. Stan Goff [Master Sergeant, US Army, Special Forces (Ret.)]. ISBN# 978-1-887128-63-6

Full Spectrum Disorder: The Military in the New American Century. Stan Goff [Master Sergeant, US Army, Special Forces (Ret.)]. ISBN# 978-1-932360-12-7

The Phoenix Program. Douglas Valentine. ISBN# 978-0-688-09130-9

Bloody Hell: The Price Soldiers Pay. Dan Hallock. ISBN# 978-0-87486-969-9

Hell, Healing, and Resistance: Veterans Speak. Daniel Hallock. ISBN# 978-0-87486-959-0

An Intimate History of Killing: Face-to-Face Killing in Twentieth-Century Warfare. Joanna Bourke. ISBN# 978-0-465-00738-7

On Killing: The Psychological Cost of Learning to Kill in War and Society. Lt. Col. Dave Grossman. ISBN# 978-0-316-04093-8

On Combat: The Psychology and Physiology of Deadly Conflict in War and in Peace. Lt. Col. Dave Grossman with Loren W. Christensen. ISBN# 978-0-9649205-4-5

Stop Teaching Our Kids to Kill: A Call to Action Against TV, Movie and Video Game Violence. Lt. Col. Dave Grossman and Gloria Degaetano. ISBN# 978-0-8041-3935-9

Internet Resource Collections

http://www.ecoccs.com/resources.html
EcoC^{2}S Resources

http://www.questionuniverse.com/resources.html
Questioning the Universe Publishing (QUP) Resources

www.ingramcontent.com/pod-product-compliance
Lightning Source LLC
Chambersburg PA
CBHW051038160426
43193CB00010B/990